JUST GET IT D.O.N.E. ALREADY!

A Simple **FRAMEWORK** that Beats Procrastination and Overwhelm by Achieving More with Less

VISHAL PATIL

First published by Ultimate World Publishing 2026
Copyright © 2026 Vishal Patil

ISBN

Paperback: 978-1-923583-40-5
Ebook: 978-1-923583-41-2

Vishal Patil has asserted his rights under the Copyright, Designs and Patents Act 1988 to be identified as the author of this work. The information in this book is based on the author's experiences and opinions. The publisher specifically disclaims responsibility for any adverse consequences which may result from use of the information contained herein. Permission to use information has been sought by the author. Any breaches will be rectified in further editions of the book.

All rights reserved. No part of this publication may be reproduced, stored in or introduced into a retrieval system, or transmitted in any form, or by any means (electronic, mechanical, photocopying, recording or otherwise) without the prior written permission of the author. Any person who does any unauthorised act in relation to this publication may be liable to criminal prosecution and civil claims for damages. Enquiries should be made through the publisher.

Cover design: Ultimate World Publishing
Layout and typesetting: Ultimate World Publishing
Editor: Marnae Kelley

Ultimate World Publishing
Diamond Creek,
Victoria Australia 3089
www.writeabook.com.au

TESTIMONIALS

"The D.O.N.E. framework gave me much needed clarity to get going. I struggled with procrastinating my goals. I did not need more advice; I needed a system. I can see myself accomplishing more without getting overwhelmed. The framework is simple and flexible and helped me arrive at solution that works for me."

- Bakul Khetkade (Artist and Entrepreneur, Vancouver, Canada)

"What makes *Just Get It D.O.N.E. Already* so powerful is the way Vishal weaves together practical tools, clear frameworks, and heartfelt storytelling. He has a rare gift for making complex psychology accessible, breaking down the barriers of procrastination and overwhelm into something readers can immediately understand and act on. The metaphors, personal reflections, and relatable stories make you feel seen in your struggles, while his framework offers a clear, actionable path forward."

- Leanne Nicole (Acting Principal, Sydney, Australia)

"The done framework is very cool. I really liked it; it provided a lot of structure to procrastination and the steps to move out of it that is adjustable for each individual."

- Jessie Kan (Marketing Specialist- Sydney, Australia)

"Working with Vishal has shown me how patient, disciplined, and insightful he is as a coach. He simplifies complex concepts and provides clear, practical guidance. I'd highly recommend him to anyone looking for a coach who makes the journey effective and inspiring."

- Deepak Seth (Account Executive, Sydney, Australia)

"Vishal is deeply passionate about helping people unlock their potential and live with clarity, confidence, and purpose. Drawing on his experiences in personal development / life lessons, Vishal combines practical strategies with heartfelt wisdom to guide people through life's challenges and opportunities. Through his work as a coach, Vishal has inspired me to embrace change, overcome setbacks, and take meaningful steps toward a more fulfilling life."

- Vinay Jain (Data architect, Sydney, Australia)

"Vishal is dedicated to helping people discover their inner strength and create meaningful change in their lives. Through his work, Vishal inspires me to overcome challenges, embrace new perspectives, and pursue a life filled with purpose and fulfillment. His approach blends timeless wisdom with actionable guidance, making personal growth both accessible and meaningful."

- Shweta Agarwal (Data Scientist, Sydney, Australia)

DEDICATION

I dedicate this book to my loving wife 'Nidhi', whose unwavering support made my dream of writing this book become a reality. This book is dedicated to my late parents who played a crucial role in letting me develop a curious mindset and helped me explore world in my own way. The book is also dedicated to my loving pet Raja for making my childhood full of loving memories and teaching that life lessons can be learned even from those not able to speak the human language.

CONTENTS

INTRODUCTION

Have you ever been in a place where you settle down, ready to start your work, and then suddenly you go blank, feeling as if something simply took away your will to do even the bare minimum?

A day when surviving without coffee felt like an impossible task? A day where you find yourself delaying things you need to do and simply end up not doing them?

That nagging feeling that despite doing so much already, you have so much more to accomplish, and you simply can't get things finished so you can have a well-deserved rest.

What if I told you that you are not alone and that it is not laziness or lethargy? These are simply symptoms of a hidden concern, a subconscious phenomenon which results in stagnation and limited productivity. We all were once cheerful kids who could spend an entire afternoon running around without thinking of the word 'fatigue'. That kid is still there somewhere, hidden beneath our awareness, raring to come out, only getting stopped because of the barriers we have created ourselves.

And you can easily make small, incremental changes to bring barriers down, releasing that energetic child again, which will make those dreadful, low-energy feelings and stagnation experiences a thing of the past.

'It is not easy, but it's very simple once you know how.' - Eric Thomas

In this book, I am sharing things that got me back to my productive ways when I lost all my motivation at the young age of 22 years. I was simply overwhelmed, staring at the ceiling, trying to find a single ounce of motivation to simply get out of the bed, having lost my father, who succumbed to a long illness, having less than $10 left in my bank account and having the responsibility to take care of my ageing mother who was suffering from heart disease. Things did not improve after that. No school or class in college taught me how to manage the human brain and get going when all you want to do is ABSOLUTELY NOTHING.

'We do not learn from experience…
we learn from reflecting on experience.'
- Commonly attributed to John Dewey

You need to learn from what has happened, understand why it happened and create long-lasting, practical solutions. You need to learn how to identify solutions that are not merely like a Band-Aid, which only covers the wound temporarily. Rather, you need solutions that tackle problems at their core, ensuring long-term and sustainable resolution. It might take few attempts to get it right. However, keep in mind...

> *If you persist, you often succeed.*

I have spent the last 15 years trying to get those answers and, in the book, I am sharing how to make your most productive self your day-to-day reality. I am an analyst who loves studying human behaviour and psychology. My qualifications as an engineer with a master's in business administration and a certified life coach have made me well equipped to capture best of both analytics and human psychology.

This book will provide you a system that creates long-lasting solutions to real-life problems through a framework I designed to simplify getting things done without unnecessary delays or procrastination. My framework is practical, it doesn't break the bank and it works. I will also provide my not-so-common analytical take on how to take on any problem (not only limited to productivity) with a clear approach and create a never-ending source of support you can use anytime: your own mind.

Our brain is an amazing organ; this blob of fat in our cranial cavity hides more secrets than the floor of the ocean (scientists claim only 5% of the world's oceans are explored and known to science). It is like a stallion who can run wild and be out of control or be trained and used in battles to fight with enemies, assisting us in winning every time. The mind is like that magician whose tricks completely astound us the first time, taking us by surprise, but once we know how the tricks are played behind the curtain, we can easily demystify its acts, removing the element of surprise.

*'The more you know where you are going,
the more likely you are to get there.'
- inspired by Stephen Covey*

The book will demystify some of the tricks our mind plays, provide you with simple but effective ways to take back control of your daily tasks and grinds and ultimately bring out your productive self every time, all the time.

So let's get it done already!

A NOTE TO READERS

Before you begin, I'd like to share something important about how to approach this book. You'll find that some parts give you the "why" behind procrastination and overwhelm, while others provide you with practical tools and methods you can start using right away. Both are important, but you don't have to master everything in one go.

The framework I share here is designed to be simple, but simplicity doesn't always mean easy. Give yourself permission to move at your own pace, to re-read when needed, and to apply only what feels most useful in the moment.

Think of this book as a guide you can return to whenever procrastination sneaks back in; a friend who want to walk with you and be a companion in your journey in beating overwhelm. And by the end, you'll see that doing more with less is not only possible—it's the most powerful way forward.

— Vishal

CHAPTER 1

FALLING BEHIND: NOT LAZY, JUST OVERLOADED

Let's be clear and extremely honest with ourselves. We know there are people who claim time management is the key to success: the better you manage your time, the more you can get done. This is the principle that was famous in the latter half of the 20th century (1950s onwards). You need to start early (early bird catches the worm), plan your day through a to-do list, categorize tasks as per priority, create an action plan and tick one task after another as you get them done.

There are multiple versions of the same knowledgebase shared through multiple books, workshops, trainings and podcasts. If it was so easy, we all would not be struggling with overwhelm and procrastination in the first place. Time management sounds good, and it's easy to sell, but it fails to account for one critical factor:

we do not live in that world anymore. We have moved on from the 20th century into a millennium where technology is running at a pace faster than any human can envision.

That was the time when technology still had physical existence, separated into different physical objects in our day-to-day lives. News came through newspapers or news bulletins on the radio or television. The main source of entertainment was limited to radio, TV or magazine. Advertisement was only limited to these few selected sources, and we could ignore them easily if we wanted. Having fun involved activities like going out with friends or family, and if you wanted to avoid socialising, you could simply refuse to participate, switch off the TV and enjoy alone time in the bedroom. Distraction, even though it still existed, could be easily tuned out.

Now we have distractions everywhere in the form of a mobile phone. Marketing agencies are trying to capture our attention every minute. We have added pressure of missing out on updates our friends are sharing if we are not online. Tuning out these distractions literally needs a detox ritual. If you asked anyone 20 years back what digital detox means, at best you would have gotten a laugh or curious question if that is some kind of new machine.

There is an entire generation of kids growing up who don't know how to eat a meal without having some form of entertainment around them. Don't believe me, just observe all the kids in shopping malls sitting with a tablet or a mobile phone in hand while the world around them goes by in a flash. A study done by Microsoft in 2015 showed the average attention span of humans has dropped from 12 seconds in the early 2000s to 8 seconds in 2015. This is similar to or less than that of a goldfish. Switching attention every few seconds has become a common phenomenon for our brains. This is not limited just to kids as mobile phone addiction is also common amongst teenagers and adults. Always feeling triggered or distracted has become a new norm, and no amount of time on hand can change how we decide to spend it.

Distractions will create an ailment, a sickness we all know by the name of 'procrastination'—an acute condition (short term) which, if not healed, will create overwhelm on regular basis, ultimately resulting in the chronic illness of burnout.

Time management may sound good but generally fails in today's world. If that was not true, even with so much knowledge on time management already available, why do we still find overwhelm and burnout a common pattern across workplaces? Time management had a good run when it actually worked in the world it was designed for. Time management, even though useful, has limited utility today, more of a placebo that works for a short period till the ailment we are facing finally catches up with us.

Time, even though it progresses at a constant rate, feels different to the human brain depending on how we feel about a task on hand. When you do something you love doing, time seems to accelerate, and when you want to target a boring task, it slows down to the point you want to run away from the torture. This results in the phenomenon where time expands to fit the deadline. If you are given 20 minutes to finish a task you do not enjoy, such as sending a report, something you know will not bring you joy, you will find yourself finishing it closer to the deadline. If the same task is given 2 hours, most probably you will finish it after 1 hour 55 minutes.

Life is full of things that need to be completed, and we are not going to enjoy all of them. No amount of time management will get us to finish the task quickly if our brain is trying to just run away from those tasks all the time. We will drop our guards down at the first hint of distraction and ultimately fall for the ailment of procrastination again.

> *Time management is a placebo.*

Yes! I said it! Time management is a good-looking and tasting medicine that makes us feel good for the time being while our deep-rooted problem becomes worse and worse. What is the point of having a lot of time on hand if we are ultimately going to waste it?

To beat procrastination and overwhelm today, you need to focus on your energy management. Succeeding in the world now has become about focusing our attention on tasks that matter, spending energy on things that count. This makes energy management and focus training the key factors to achieve your goals.

Procrastination's Hidden Agenda

'Procrastination is like a credit card: It's a lot of fun until you get the bill.' - Christopher Parker

Procrastination is nothing but a decision to not do what needs to be done now. The tricky part here is we don't make this decision consciously every time. There are hidden factors most of us are not even aware of. They play a crucial part in making us choose delay tactics over action. If I use the neuroscience term, then I can say that procrastination originates due to subconscious reasons.

I remember when I was working on a project, I had a stakeholder who I did not get along with very well. I was part of a wider team with interdependent responsibilities, and this individual (let's call this person Penelope) would always act as if the world was on fire and everything would go down the drain if Penelope's priorities were not acted upon right away. Even when the rest of the team obliged, there was new drama all the time. Once I had a big tussle for priorities, and Penelope, being in her usual 'house on fire' mode, got preference from management, leading to delay in my side of work. To compensate for lost time, I had to spend my weekend completing the tasks which could have been finished during the regular working time. If it was one instance, I would have ignored it, but somehow this repeated a few more times, and over the years I developed a natural hate towards Penelope's approach of getting her priorities met by creating unnecessary drama.

Then came a moment where part of the project depended on me, and the person who was going to benefit from it was Penelope. All those days of frustration crept in, and I made every attempt to delay this part, using all my might. It was revenge because no amount of 'house on fire' tactics was going to work on me this time. I was ready to face any form of escalation. Ultimately, I got my revenge, giving me a sense of depraved satisfaction. I only finished my part when escalation reached a point in hierarchy I could no longer ignore, and by that time my urge to get revenge was satisfied. Was it good for the overall team? No! But it was my revenge.

This was an example where I consciously procrastinated, actively delayed action by refusing to finish what was needed. But if you look deeper, our brain does this to us all the time. Scientists call it revenge procrastination. We delay doing what we need to do because there are hidden factors stopping us from getting things done. The most common factors are the following:

- **Emotions:** If you don't like doing something, maybe getting out of bed early in the morning or taking out trash, washing dishes, writing boring reports, etc., you will find you avoid it because in the past those activities have not treated you well reward-wise, and you got the punishment of boredom. This causes a natural aversion within your brains as these tasks trigger negative emotions attached to your previous experience. So, when you are expected to do it again, your emotions take revenge and you stop or delay what needs to be done, unless the things escalate to a certain level.

- **Self-doubt:** If you think that you are not good enough to get it done, you might use avoidance strategies to procrastinate. For instance, playing guitar was my dream for such a long time but just because I could not see myself getting good at it, I hesitated in giving it a go. Even when I joined classes and took few lessons, I was usually embarrassed to see others making so much progress and myself getting left behind. Ultimately, my self-doubt reinforced itself and I stopped going to classes altogether. Sometimes self-doubt stops you from taking the first step, and sometimes it creates hurdles, making progress almost impossible.

- **Mood:** We just don't feel like doing it. Our mood can throw a tantrum like a toddler in a candy store. Let's say you have decided to do something critical but not fun at 10 pm. At 9:57 pm your mood will try to persuade you to organize your socks drawer, have a snack or simply wander off in fond memories of that fun event that happened last month, anything that will distract you from getting started on actual work. This is also referred to as present bias, which means doing something fun now over something critical or important as the mood is not aligned with what needs to be done. So instead of facing that awkward, uncomfortable feeling head on, we end up chasing mood boosts, like social media scrolling or eating chips straight out of a bag or simply staring out of the window for no apparent reason.

- **Perfectionism:** Some of us are just born with a tendency to do everything as if it is going to get evaluated and if we do not get a perfect score, it's a failure. This is a perfectionism trap. We set high standards for ourselves, and this will prevent us from finishing the task at hand and moving on to other tasks, irrespective of how crucial that task is.

- **'Hang on' effect:** I coined it myself. Sometimes you fall in love with something so much that you just want to keep doing it. The activity brings so much joy that everything else feels meaningless, and therefore you stick with it way beyond the time needed or allocated. Saying 'Hang on' to every other task till you are satisfied with the one you enjoy.

- **Inner clock neuroscience:** Every human has a built-in sense of time. There are two types of personalities: through-time and in-time. In-time people have a less synchronised internal clock with a tendency to lose track of time. Once they are in the zone, they simply forget the concept of time, spending hours on something that should have been completed a long time ago. Switching tasks is very difficult for these types of personalities. On the other hand, through time people have a weird sense of time (me included). We always know what time it is and can accurately estimate how many minutes are remaining, especially when we are running late. We are those crazy people who will make a big fuss about missing trains or flights or being late. Procrastination can affect both these personalities. In-time people get lost in the task and forget to move on, while through-time personalities will keep tasks unfinished if not done on time, leading to delayed finish and ultimately procrastination.

(Note: biological reasons are also responsible for procrastination, and as they are medically driven, they're outside of my expertise and therefore not discussed in detail in this book.)

Whatever may be the reason for the procrastination, we must understand it is a choice. The first step in overcoming any obstacle is to understand there exists one. Procrastination may present itself in any of the following stages of task:

- **Starting:** This is generally affected by delay tactics or emotional reasons. The avoidance strategy is at its best here.

- **Maintaining:** The present bias plays a very big role here. The moment things start becoming boring and mood starts getting affected, the tendency to jump to something that is rewarding takes over and we fail to maintain the progress in the task.

- **Finishing:** Perfectionism and the 'hang on' effect can make us not see the finish line, even though we could easily reach it.

Overwhelm Is a Symptom

As kids, most of us only needed to be worried about maybe three or four things like studies, friends and not getting into an accident. Having plenty of time and energy, we breeze through our days. There are guidance and instructions provided, and most of our decisions are made for us. As we grow, life seems to go fast, becoming more complex and filled with variables that were missing earlier. We have work life, personal life, relationships to maintain, a body that needs to be kept healthy, a mind that needs to be trained and upgraded, and after managing all these we're supposed to somehow get relaxation and fun as everything else will fall apart if we don't rejuvenate.

There is a long list of things that need to be done, responsibilities to be handled, wealth to be earned and life to be lived. So much with the same amount of time every day. The more we fall behind, the longer the list grows.

This is not a scary movie; it's a reality, the story of every responsible individual who wants to play the game of life. No escape. You are part of it now, and whether you plan it well or not, it does not stop. Getting to grow up to be an adult is a privilege, getting to grow to an old age even more so. In human evolution, over the centuries, the average life expectancy has steadily increased, and it has almost doubled in the last few decades.

Earlier, in nomadic tribes, we were responsible for hunting and gathering food. Every day, humans had to fight against natural elements like predators, weather and rival tribes to survive. We had to be always on alert from the real-life threatening danger. Our brains got designed to be in fight or flight mode whenever our safety was threatened. Evolution is a slow process, and therefore even after centuries passed, our body and brain still have not gotten rid of those danger-sensing habits. This tendency is controlled by our primitive or reptilian brain, called the amygdala. It triggers when we sense danger. Now we don't hunt for food; rather, we are purchasing it from the shelves of supermarkets or ordering online. The danger of getting attacked by a tiger doesn't exist anymore. However, that reptilian part of our brain still alerts us that our life is in danger without any pertinent risk of physical harm. The risk now is of failing in our responsibilities, losing self-worth or social approval.

The brain doesn't understand this difference and will trigger the same stress signal which puts us on high alert. The stress signals then cause us to stay high on adrenaline, also known as epinephrine. It is a hormone and neurotransmitter that prepares the body for the fight or flight response, triggering physiological changes like increased heart rate, blood pressure, and blood flow to muscles, while also decreasing pain sensitivity. As adrenaline drops, the energy consumed during rush and stress takes its toll, making us tired and slow.

When we are not doing what needs to be done, it is only natural that tasks and responsibilities keep adding up, eventually getting us to a level of stress where functioning normally becomes almost impossible. This is called overwhelm.

Remember, having too many responsibilities is like having too many tabs open on our computer browser. It overloads our systems, making us slow and exhausted. Sometimes whatever we do, we still fall behind, and that overwhelm creeps in. Our brain still triggers it as a stress signal and creates that flight or fight response, eventually making us tired when adrenaline keeps coming up and going away.

When overwhelm sticks around long enough, it not only makes us slow or tired, but it also acts like a wildfire encroaching closer and closer to our entire neighbourhood, which after a particular point creates burnout. It never happens suddenly; it is a slow process. The World Health Organization mentions burnout as 'chronic workplace stress that has not been successfully managed'. This also affects our brain in the long run.

Remember when you marinate your brain with overwhelm for a long time, burnout is the final dish.

The good news is, when we know how the fire operates and travels, we can take precautions to avoid wildfire. We need to be strategic where we create barriers and stop the fuel. Overwhelm can be averted if we know when to stop feeding the fire, something we will cover in detail when we discuss the D.O.N.E. framework.

Remember the main reason why overwhelm happens is not because things are difficult; it's because we are not doing what needs to be done. We need to realise our responsibilities in terms of the tasks and activities do not become less overtime. In fact, it is the other way around. They grow with time. The best way to tackle them is to do these two things:

1. Prepare ourselves to handle more.
2. Learn to stop the overwhelm spread.

Continuing with the fire analogy, we need to keep in mind that wet grass takes more time to catch fire than dry grass. We need to keep our pasture green and thriving. Same is with our brain and body. We need to take care of ourselves, and as the responsibilities grow, we should be well prepared and equipped with handling what is expected of us.

'It is not easy, but it's very simple once you know how.' - Eric Thomas

Mindset is a keyword that comes in use while trying to manage mental fatigue and overwhelm. It is a great thing, but if you try to learn it from gurus who say they have got it all sorted through a quick fix and one-solution-fits-all approach, you are most likely in for a disappointment. What you need is sustainable framework, which is customised for individual needs, simple to follow and aligned with what works for you. Not a quick fix Band-Aid solution but a strategic approach through a well-built system that makes you grow stronger as things gets tougher and more challenging.

People who go to the gym or work out regularly know that the body is not built while working out or in the gym. In fact, exercising breaks the muscle fibres in the form of microtears, which are built back when we are resting with the help of nourishment like proteins and vitamins. Also, you cannot build your body by going to gym once for ten hours; it is done by following regular structured steps with consistent effort and discipline.

Similarly, for ensuring you overcome and sustainably stay away from the ailments of procrastination and overwhelm, you need an approach that requires a structured framework, consistent effort and sustainable actions that help you not only survive the journey called life but thrive and excel at it.

We are in this for a long haul, not a hit-and-run approach. War is not won by one who hits hardest but one who survives to flourish at the end. In the next chapter we will discuss how analytics can be used to solve the problem of procrastination and overwhelm, the importance of framework and how to look at life in simple way to tackle the problem of procrastination and overwhelm.

In short

1. Time management is often ineffective in today's world due to multiple distractions caused by advanced technology, social media and changing work-life dynamics.
2. Procrastination is not always a result of laziness; it is caused by multiple factors such as emotions, self-doubt, mood, perfectionism, the "Hang-on" effect and inner-clock neuroscience.
3. Procrastination can occur at the stages of starting, maintaining or finishing tasks.
4. Overwhelm is a symptom that, if not treated, can lead to burn-out.
5. You need structured framework, consistent and sustainable effort in the right direction to get over procrastination and stop overwhelm.

CHAPTER 2

A DIFFERENT PERSPECTIVE: AN ANALYTICAL TAKE ON LIFE

Let me take you back to the time in history when mathematics and analytics were done through words and not as we know them today. Mathematics is a precise language comprising symbols and equations. We have calculators that provide options of so many functions to be performed just by using few selected keys, and they rarely require detailed instructions. In ancient times, solving mathematical equation was more like telling a story. Instead of writing 1+1 = 2, sentences were used, such as 'If we add one thing to one more thing, we get two things, which doubles the available thing'. In that world dominated by verbal and descriptive transmission, this method had merit as it ensured transfer of knowledge without reliance of written format; paper was scarce and expensive to produce.

However, verbal transmission could lead to ambiguity and misinterpretation. As the mathematics became more complex, including quadratic and other expressions, symbols were used to note mathematical equations, which made it easy to write and interpret. It was acknowledged globally as it overcame language barriers.

Overwhelm happens when our computing system (a.k.a. brain) is flooded with too many variables, some real and some imaginary, too many emotional noises and the absence of a clear sequence of steps to arrive at a solution. Our brains get cluttered with our thoughts, which are easily influenced by our emotions and hidden subconscious biases and interferences. It becomes difficult to express and identify the problems as a first step before we can get solving and moving ahead through needed actions. Filters are lacking, and mental clutter follows; the brain becomes overloaded, consuming too much energy and at times halting the processing of data, resulting in a state of no progress. This is similar to early stages of mathematical equations, cluttered in too many words, open for interpretation and possible ambiguity, before the framework of symbols existed to make it simple to interpret and solve.

When you procrastinate, remember you are driven by an emotional paragraph freezing you instead of structural clarity and a symbolic framework to drive the action. The D.O.N.E framework is your mental translation tool, which will not say 'Just do it' by giving you one solution guaranteeing that all your problems will be solved. Instead, it provides clarity in chaos, sorts the signals from noise and makes solving the problem simpler by focusing on action through one clear step at time. Remember, we are all unique combinations of multiple variables at play. Even twins have different tendencies when going about their lives.

Three Key Variables

If you look at life in a simpler sense, there are only three key variables at play at any point of time:

1. **Variable T (controllable time)**: We all get 24 hours in a day. The only variable here is the amount of time we have control over. This is a crazy paradox. Here when I refer to variable T, it does not refer to 24 hours in a day but the time we can control as per our needs.

2. **Variable R**: Our ability to gain and use resources, also called wealth. Money, in itself, is nothing. It is a transaction medium that allows us to gain resources for our living. This includes how can we go about earning wealth, either through salary gained in a job, profits through a business or payments received through royalties, interests and our skill sets. The variable R refers to our ability to gain resources.

3. **Variable E**: How much energy we need to spend to do what needs to be done, synonymous with our mental and emotional Health. This indicates our daily vigour and peak efficiency.

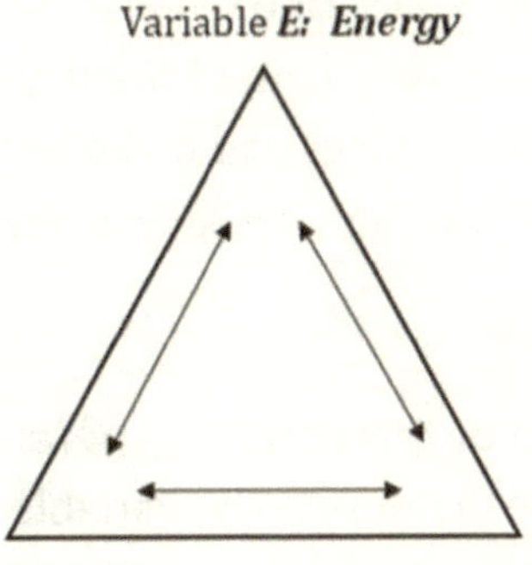

The balance between these three variables creates a baseline for maximizing the throughput of life. Whether you are working in a job or handling your own business, typically these three variables play out as below.

When you are young, you rely on your parents and guardians to provide resources necessary for your survival. You are dependent on others to decide how you use those resources (low on **variable R).** On the other hand, you have your entire life ahead of you and limited responsibilities needing time commitment (high on **variable T).** The day seems to never end, and every meal fills you up with ample amount of energy to play and move around for hours, so much so you can skip meals and feel nothing (high on **variable E**).

As you grow into your young-adult self, your ability to gain resources **(variable R)** increases based on your skillset and physical ability. Your youthful self is also high on energy **(variable E)** so much so that only few hours of sleep is enough to carry you throughout your days and still give you enough vitality to survive. The only thing you do find rushing for is **(variable T)** time you have control over. You have so much to do and so much to learn. The harder you push yourself, the more responsibilities get added, and typically variable R improves as you are rewarded for handling the demand of the new responsibilities. This is generally the case for your entire working life (between 18 years to 65 years). The variable E is the major challenge here as the demand of the day-to-day grind takes its toll on your vigour. The choices you make here determines how variable E will play out. However, it is also a variable which is most neglected.

As you reach an age of retirement, generally the variable R is good and variable T also increases. The variable E is on the decline as physical health deteriorates with age. The fruits of your labour are provided to you, and whether you can enjoy them is completely dependent on how strong and functioning your teeth still are.

The Notion of Productivity and Accomplishment

The definition of the word *productivity* has changed a lot in the last few decades. In the industrial age, how many units per measure of time were produced was considered productivity. This was easy to measure and could be easily benchmarked. If a factory employed 100 workers who each produced 10 pieces per hour, at the end of 8-hour working day, 10 multiplied by 100 multiplied by 8, which equals 8000 pieces, becomes the target. Any shortfall from this number meant the factory was not producing at 100%. This was same in project terms as well. If a unit (e.g. building construction) needed 100 workers working for 90 days and they completed the building in 90 days, you get 100% productivity. Each worker could be held accountable for work performed or units produced per unit of time and paid accordingly for the number of hours they worked. This was easy to measure and replicate through automation.

As the time went on and the information age took over, the measure of productivity became more blurred. The evolving technology made working faster and decreased the time required to perform a unit of work. Sometimes, those units of measure keep changing as well. One measure is often not enough to identify productivity. Working from home makes it even more difficult. An employee working for eight hours needs to perform multiple tasks, not all of those resulting in tangible output that could be measured and quantified. The higher you are in the ladder, the vaguer your work measurement becomes. In fact, having conflicting priorities has become a norm, where different teams are given different objectives, causing friction. The conflicts are not only accepted;

they are expected. The new normal made it even more difficult to measure how productive an employee is. Some tasks could be finished in minutes while others seem never ending.

The sense of accomplishment and resulting satisfaction has become subjective. This has resulted in a situation where switching off from work requires conscious decision. International borders and cross-continent projects have even blurred what working hours look like. Not every day can be planned in the buckets between 9 am to 5 pm. The time, which flows at a constant rate, has become a variable **(variable T)**.

The more complex the world has become, the more artificial variables, also known as performance indicators, have been introduced. The monthly, quarterly and annual performances now dictate rates of success and failure. A worker who is not even involved in key decision-making faces repercussions and prospects of loss of employment because downsizing is the fastest way to meet the expected bottom-line. As an individual, the challenges you face are not limited on how good you are in your work; they are beyond visible horizon.

The human brain cannot differentiate between what is real and what is imaginary. When you are dreaming, everything looks real. Every imaginary danger becomes threatening. The dreamworld becomes your entire existence. Similarly, when work-related responsibilities take over most of your life, it is very easy to get lost in the notion that your success as an employee or a business owner is directly related to your success overall.

Our human brains love clarity, and the lifelong questions 'who are we?' and 'what is our purpose?' become muddled in the responsibilities of work and profession. People attach their personal status and significance to the designation they hold in an organization and the revenue their business generates. The sense of accomplishment gets directly linked to the material reward and ability to gain resources (**variable R).** The common mistake many amongst us are guilty of committing is ignoring how **variable E** is playing out.

The Quest for More

'How to get rich quickly?' is the question many wants to know the answer to. The passive income concept is entirely based on maximizing variable R while not affecting variable T. I am not saying it's a bad thing or not acceptable. The concept of time management is focused on managing variable T (ability to use time) while the variable R (ability to gain resources) is the centre of existence. The concern that most individuals face is how to gain more wealth by maximizing utility of our time. Accomplish more to achieve more has become a mantra of sorts. The focus is to balance variable T with variable R.

With limited focus on variable E (our energy levels), no wonder the balance between the three variable is skewed. I am not saying being ambitious or growth minded is a bad thing; maximizing time utility and increasing a wealth aspect are both noble endeavours, if done well and with strategic thinking.

Work-life balance does not mean spending 50% of your time at work and 50% away from it. It means how we are able to balance these three variables by not compromising on any. The best time to do that is during our working age, and the best way to do it is by focusing on all three variables. Not having enough energy while maximizing other two variables is like having the world's most luxurious car with no fuel.

So, the important questions we need to address becomes this: 'How can we ensure the variable E stays flourishing while we focus on variable T and variable R?'

There are two basic principles you need to keep in mind when you are adopting an analytical mindset in life and while approaching any situation or problem.

1. If there is a problem, there must be a solution

If a problem exists, there must be a way to solve it. If you are not aware of one in the present moment, doesn't mean it doesn't exist. Also, when you focus on progress over perfection, there is more than one way to solve the same problem.

When you are operating in survival mode, it's easy for your brain to get filled with unnecessary emotions and fears. This freezes you from making any progress, and you get lost in the emotional stories. 'If' and 'but' become louder. A cornered cat will only react with fight, flight or freeze. This knee-jerk reaction makes solving problems more difficult than they ever need to be. If it is not a real life-threatening situation, don't react like one. Repeat to yourself:

If there is a problem, there must be a solution.

2. Evidence over assumption

The human brain hates gaps in knowledge and will always try to fill these gaps, even if those gaps are filled incorrectly with assumptions. Do not jump to a conclusion as it stops any critical thinking. For example, if someone does not like going to the gym, do not assume that person is lazy or the person simply lacks motivation. If you go with assumptions as a first step, you are more likely to search for evidence that only validates your assumptions and reject anything that is not aligned with it. Remember your subconscious biases, filters, values (discussed in detail in Chapter 4) and belief system are always at play, and your brain will jump to adopt the path of least resistance through falling back on available information and thoughts. This will hinder any progress, resulting in the same old patterns. Be aware and look for substantial evidence before you draw any conclusions.

As a kid I had a pet dog named Raja, and he loved running around the house and field. He had strong build with a coarse voice and a smart brain. At the time, I lived in a village named Nachangaon in central part of India with my family. Electrical supply back then in India was intermittent.

During the nights without electricity, it used to get really dark. Living near a farm and surrounded by farm animals, we always shut the main door, and Raja did not like it at all. He would bark outdoors and other dogs in the vicinity would join the chorus. One such night when it got dark with no electricity, we realised Raja was barking again, and this was mostly ignored by all of us, but after persistent barking and some scratching on the door, my grandfather got curious. On further investigation, he saw Raja running between a water tank on the ground and the main door and barking all the way repeatedly.

My grandfather, a very old man, carried his torch and went outside the main gate to investigate Raja's unusual behaviour. He tracked down Raja and observed that a calf had fallen into the water tank and Raja was barking to raise an alarm. Raja's intelligence and my grandfather's curiosity saved the calf from drowning that night.

If my grandpa would have just ignored Raja's barking as a regular thing rather than investigating, a life would have been lost. You never know what you will find in investigation, so go with an open, curious mind and don't jump to conclusions. Investigate before arriving at a conclusion and don't assume as it may be detrimental to getting a solution that works.

Our human brains thrive on clarity. When we know which direction we need to progress, the end goal and the steps, the decision making becomes simple and can be done quickly in a manner that is repetitive and sustainable. We live in an era where knowledge is available, easily accessible. This also leads to overload of information. Too many choices actually make you slow and increases the probability of you choosing lucrative quick solutions over more impactful ones. We are all a unique combination of skillset, experience, learnings, values (discussed in detail in Chapter 4), beliefs. Trying to adopt a method that does not align with our way of living can stop the effectiveness and impact of the adopted method, techniques and steps. Therefore, our uniqueness needs to be celebrated and utilised. This can be accomplished using D.O.N.E. framework.

Before we learn the D.O.N.E framework in detail, it is also essential to understand how to maximize variable E in day-to-day life. In the next chapter, I will discuss how to maximize our day-to-day energy level, the charge in the battery that keeps you going.

In short

1. Too many emotions can clutter your thinking and cause confusion leading to overwhelm.
2. There are three key variables at play at any time: Variable E (your energy level), variable T (controllable time) and Variable R (your ability to gain resources).
3. You need to focus on maximizing all three variables.
4. Two basic principles for adopting an analytical mindset:
    a. If there is a problem, there must be a solution.
    b. Seek evidence over assumption.

CHAPTER 3

THE KEY CURRENCY: ENERGY, NOT TIME

You get 86,400 seconds in a day. Whether you like it or not, you cannot get more, and you cannot get less. The only choice or variable you have is to decide how you spend it.

Let's say you are talking to a young kid who is just starting to have a side hustle to make his pocket money. It simply makes sense to pay the kid based on the work the kid performs, the amount of energy and focus the kid spends on completing the activity handed over to him. And the kid is paid at the end of the day. Based on his need for pocket money, a kid will work towards completing tasks that maximize the amount he receives by the end of the day. There is a high chance if the kid is focusing on buying something worthwhile (like a big goal), the kid will spend more energy and effort on tasks with high reward.

Now assume an alternate scenario. The kid is going to get $100 in his hands every day at the start of the day, whether he works or not. Do you think the kid is going to spend his energy on tasks now or just go around using money for whatever activity interests him? Will the kid even worry about money? The motivation will simply be lacking. The only time the kid will get worried is if the money is taken away or he is restricted from spending it till the time he has finished the allocated work.

That is real life for you. We get the same amount of time allocated to us every day at the start (86,400 seconds). It is not about managing time but on what we spend energy on. How we look at the reward at the end, and are driven to achieve it, will determine where our focus is throughout our day. The true challenge lies not in scheduling every minute, but in directing our limited mental and emotional energy toward goals that truly matter.

There are multiple factors at play that affect our life choices on a day-to-day basis. Some are evident while some are hidden. Some of these factors and underlying reasons are provided below

- **Not all days are same**

We are humans, not machines who can be designed to work at the same rhythm and energy level always. We need to acknowledge that not every hour of the day or every day of the week is the same. If you are a morning person, you may find you are able to get more done earlier in the day than at the latter part of the day, and the reverse will happen if you are a night owl. We need to remember our energy level is dependent on multiple factors, such as what nourishment we had (a hungry mind is an angry mind), what our surroundings are (is it causing friction and stopping us from being efficient or completely focused on our work?) and what emotional state we are in. We might see within a single day that we go through different phases, some where we are super active and others where we just want to crash and rest.

Even the rest doesn't mean the same thing for all of us; some want to sit down in the corner alone and have a moment of peace, while others love to chat to their friends or loved ones to gain back energy. This variety makes us unique; there is no one size that fits all. If you have kids, you might have seen every kid operates at a different energy level. Some are hyper while others have a gentle rhythm. This is our natural rhythm. Years of schooling and training have made us forget our rhythms, and we are expected to behave like machines when it comes to work and responsibilities. That is not natural and, therefore, doesn't work for all. Identifying your natural rhythm is the first step in getting best out of your day.

• Having free time does not equal productivity

Many have wish lists like learning to play an instrument, get good at an adventure sport, consistently pursue a hobby, travel the world and others. However, we failed to do so as life and responsibilities got in the way. When COVID lockdown happened, many of us stopped travelling to work, and we gained back time we used to spend on our daily commute. This would have meant we could finally do what we always wanted to do: learn to play guitar, do yoga or exercise at home, write that book, catch up with our long-lost contacts. And if social media is to be trusted, many of us started doing it. However, it soon dwindled away, and most of us were back to living normal lives. Time was not a problem here; it was available, but those items on the wish list kept pending. This indicates that the lack of time is not the main reason we are not doing what we need and want to do. It has to do with our choices and our focus.

• Energy Vampires

Energy vampires are the activities, thoughts and emotions that causes unnecessary friction and are hidden reasons why you feel tired and lose focus on the critical actions. These are primary reasons why even with best intentions and preparation, you are not able to make intended progress towards your goals and fall behind. They can manifest in these forms:

a. Distractions

Distractions show up in different ways, and when you don't recognize them, they quietly drain away your energy and attention, affecting your Variable E and also Variable T. Here are many types of distractions that may come up:

- External distractions such as noises and interruptions
- Internal distractions such as random thoughts or worries
- Social distractions such as demands, requests and interactions from others that interrupt your flow
- Digital distractions such as endless pings, scrolling and app hopping that fragment focus
- Physical distractions such as fatigue, hunger, discomfort or lack of concentration
- Opportunity distractions such as new ideas or shiny projects that tempt you away from current priorities

b. Contingencies

Contingencies are the unexpected events, conditions or obstacles that arise, which influence the way we work. They are the 'what ifs' and unplanned scenarios that can slow progress, create uncertainty and affect variable E. Contingencies change the conditions you must work within. Here are many types of contingencies:

- Time contingencies such as unexpected delays, last-minute changes or deadlines shifting
- Dependency contingencies such as waiting on someone else's input, approval or actions due to co-dependencies or working in a team environment; also conflicts, miscommunication or demands from others
- Health contingencies such as illness, fatigues or accidents causing injury
- Environment contingencies such as changes in your surroundings like noise, weather or workspace limitations
- Resource contingencies such as lack of access to tools, critical resources or information not available when needed

c. Clutter

Clutter refers to the excesses in the form of either physical, digital or mental nature. They occupy space and waste energy. They are discussed in detail in Chapter 8.

It is necessary to look for energy vampires as they tend to reduce our variable E like a leakage in the water tank draining our energy and limiting progress.

• Natural behaviour versus nurtured behaviour

When we are born, we do not know how to use words to communicate with others. Our language skill is limited to crying, smiling, facial expressions or making random noises. It takes many months before we can speak our first word. The language skills we develop rely on the environment and people surrounding us during our upbringing. That's learned or nurtured behaviour. However, we have a natural rhythm of sleeping, feeding, and if we ask our parents, they will tell us we had a dominant emotion (for instance happy baby, cry-baby, clingy baby, independent baby, etc.), which constitutes our natural behaviour. Over the years we learn to adapt to our surroundings through the influences we have such as our parents, siblings, friend circle and teachers, and due to this, we ultimately evolve to be an adult who prefers to behave in a certain way.

If a behaviour can be learned, it can also be unlearned. If some behavioural patterns that we have adopted through years of training (conscious or unconscious) are not serving us, we can unlearn them, and this is the good news. Remember, nobody was born with a job title; we earn it, and we can always adapt and change. 'I have always been like this' is not a true statement. We have a choice, a choice to adapt and change or stay as we are. There is no fix way of doing things or pattern that cannot be broken.

• Peak performance period

Science has proven that our performance peak occurs at different times of the day. Even our hormones change throughout the day and are also dependent on the activities we perform. Testosterone (needed for physical tasks and exercise) will shoot up in the morning and will fluctuate throughout the day. Our body and mind have a natural rhythm and variation; therefore, we need to align and understand what our peak performance time zone is and learn to utilize it.

Here, I would love to emphasize the fact that we sometimes waste time and energy without even recognizing it. What differentiates the human species from other animals and trees is our ability to choose. Remember, we always have a choice, and things happen due to actions that may or may not be consciously known to us. When we are not having enough time and energy, it means we are spending time on activities that are not serving us or making choices that drain our energy, ultimately making us slow.

'Time is a created thing. To say,
"I don't have time" is to say, "I don't want to."'
- Lao Tzu

I will use an example of working out in the gym. I have seen people finishing their workout in 60 minutes and others spending 90 minutes, and I have seen it have the same effect on fitness based on my own personal experience. The reason is generally recovery time between sets. Whenever I take my mobile phone with me into the gym and have a headset, I will make sure I am listening to a good song to keep me motivated throughout the workout. If the wrong playlist or song plays, I will stop the workout and correct it and also might check for any notifications before I restart the workout. Then one day my mobile phone just stopped working: screen went blank and would not reboot. I took it in for repairs, and since it was going to be repaired within a few hours I didn't bother to take a replacement phone to the gym. I work out like normal; the only difference is that I was done 30 minutes earlier and felt the same effect on the body at the end. I also realized that the songs played in the gym speakers are not bad, and even if I didn't like any song, I was working out with same rigour and intensity. The unnecessary obligation of having the correct song play made me slower. Also, no notifications meant no losing track of resting time between sets, making me stick to the workout routine and rest interval better.

You are wasting time without even knowing it. There is so much to do, and the task list keeps growing. The filler activities are distracting you from sticking to the rhythm and state of getting things completed. Because when you switch tasks, there is a lag, called residue effect, carried from one task to another. The best way to avoid this is by managing your energy and focus. Eventually, time will take care of itself as an outcome. You are not out of time but simply not focusing your energy on the right things and wasting it by spending it on non-essential activities. What you need to do is practice better energy management.

So, what is energy management? This is not a technical term for energy running the furnace or generating electricity. Here energy management means ensuring we design our activities and perform tasks in a way that keeps our energy reserve always full or near full, gaining energy from the work we do and achieving results without getting burnt out. So how do you achieve it?

1. Focus the energy

Solar energy is scattered all around us. It is necessary for generating food for plants through photosynthesis, it helps our skin generate vitamin D and it can also help in creating electricity through solar panels. Sunlight is essential for life and sustenance. However, the same sun rays sent through magnifying glass can create a concentrated beam of light so intense, it can burn the leaf instead of creating food. You can create the same effect in your life by using focus as a concentrating glass for your energy.

'Your focus determines your reality.'
- the character of Qui-Gon Jinn from the
Star Wars film The Phantom Menace.

If you focus on the task at hand and not the distractions, getting things done on time or even before becomes simple. Focusing on one thing, just like sunlight, can stop you from wasting energy on unnecessary distractions like a gym playlist. How we can achieve that focus is something I will cover in the Chapter 7 in detail.

2. Fun is the secret sauce

Find any kid who loves playing with toys. They will willingly spend hours doing it without getting even slightly tired. Ask the same kid to collect his toys from the floor, and he would be exhausted. The toys remain the same; what changes is the amount of fun the kid gets out of that activity. Same with you. You need to learn to have fun while doing what you need to do. The most boring tasks can be made to feel like a vacation if there is an intention to make it fun. Your mind is amazing. The way you react to things makes your mind generate resultant emotional reactions, not the other way around. You need to train your subconscious to start having fun while performing tasks. The way to do it is discussed in the Chapter 9 in detail.

3. Micro-breaks

A human brain can perform at a peak level for a few minutes at a time; after that, performance starts to dwindle. For most of us, it is somewhere between 45 minutes to 90 minutes. After this, the energy required to maintain the performance keeps on increasing. This is the time for a short break, lasting two to five minutes. This break should be just enough time to get a glass of water, take a simple walk, stretch or enjoy a quick view of the sky—whatever helps you get your energy back. The blob of fat called the brain just has 2% body mass but consumes 20% of your energy. To keep it active at the peak level, giving it a small time to recharge is a must.

You can't pour from an empty cup.

Keep refilling the cup in between; don't wait for it to become completely dry. That's when burnout happens.

Even though some of these actions looks simple in nature, your legacy thinking and lifelong subtle training stop you from doing it.

You might think that you are too old to change now; you have been trained to grind and get things done whether you like it or not. How can you change it suddenly?

Well, you don't need to change everything all at once. Remember a small change can create spark, which will generate momentum for things to happen later. Start with one small thing. Years' worth of unlearning cannot be done in a day, but it can be done. Remember, there are people who learned how to drive a car and earned their driving license at the age of 35 years. Yes, it was me. That is not an achievement, just a note that you can always get started and change what needs to be changed. Take one habit that you know for sure needs to be altered, something that qualifies as an energy vampire and start working on it.

For instance, some people think healthy food is an investment and they do not have enough money. Here, if you can't replace your less healthy food options with healthier versions, identify things that can be eliminated. Stop taking sugar in tea or coffee, replace cream milk with non-cream milk. Replace donuts with muesli for breakfast. Replace chips with salad. You don't need to break the bank; just replace what is unnecessary with a good alternative.

So, to maximize your energy, identify your peak part of the day and reserve most critical task for that time. Remember everyone is unique. We have different rhythms. If you are most creative in the morning, block out mornings for the tasks that require critical thinking, and shift all meetings to the afternoon. If you do not have authority to do that, then have a conversation with a person who can make that decision. When you are working in natural rhythm, your performance will improve. Leverage it to excel. Also, stop buying groceries from the ultra-processed food aisle. This is easy. Make it a point to avoid this lane. If it's not easy, ask someone to do groceries for you or just order online. Fast food will make you slow. Eliminate it or replace it.

If you think you are too busy to work out or have no time for working out, you can make small changes: take stairs instead of escalators or elevators, stretch every 90 minutes, don't use a car for distances less than 1 km; walk instead. Small changes are all it takes to get moving. Decide the activity, which is easy to incorporate in life, and stick with it. These small things add up to create a big impact.

Remember, we are not machines; we have natural rhythms and strength. Maximizing energy does not take much. It needs you to start small, build momentum and keep making necessary and sustainable changes.

In short

1. Multiple factors cause us to not utilise our time efficiently such as energy vampires, our choices and focus, our natural behaviour versus nurtured behaviour and peak performance period.
2. To maximise your daily work efficiency, you need to
   a. Focus your energy on high impact tasks.
   b. Add fun to make tasks fill effortless.
   c. Take micro-breaks to maintain peak performance levels.
   d. Maximize your daily energy levels through small and incremental life changes.

CHAPTER 4

THE D.O.N.E. FOUNDATION: CLARITY AND MOMENTUM

I want to introduce to you the D.O.N.E. Framework. Let me be honest: it is not a magic formula or a rigid productivity hack but an outcome of my own need to get clarity during moments when life felt too much, and I was left looking for guidance. One thing I realized in over 16 years in my career is that what makes any job or task simple is to have clarity on what needs to be done, how it needs to be done and your ability to gain support in making progress when you are stuck. The skillset develops over time, but support is something that needs to be present if you need to accelerate your progress. When you start from scratch, thinking takes up the most amount of energy. Figuring out things has its benefits, but it is generally a time-consuming process. You are already rushing to achieve more and do more as you try to juggle personal and professional responsibility. It is like trying to assemble a cupboard purchased from Ikea without instructions. You will get there eventually, but you'll spend a lot of time and energy figuring out stuff.

What makes the D.O.N.E. framework especially helpful in today's world is that it is not about task management or time management but focuses on one thing that is always with you: support from your own mind. It is not about pushing harder but making things simple enough for you to ensure you get busy living without running out of gas. This approach helps you build momentum, a way to re-centre, rest, develop support systems and make doing things feel almost effortless. You won't have a hundred sticky notes, a perfect routine or six productivity apps to make it work. It is designed to reduce decision fatigue, maximize personal energy and take the word 'grind' out of your day-to-day life.

The framework is a guide that, when implemented, helps you identify and leverage your uniqueness and create solutions which are made by you for you.

I personally believe comparison should be done with the self, and benchmarking can be done with others. The goals can be same, but steps to reach those goals can be your own creation. The D.O.N.E framework makes exactly that happen. It is based on the following fundamentals:

• Clarity comes from within

No amount of guidance, information, teaching and lessons is going to change how you live your life until you decide to make the necessary changes by taking the actions needed. This is where motivation fails. Motivation, when present, can act as a propeller that launches rockets in the stratosphere. However, when it's not present, pushing yourself to do what is necessary can feel like a drag. It needs conscious effort and decision on your part to keep moving. Until and unless you know that you are in control of the decisions you make and take full responsibility, life feels like a series of events happening to you, a movie whose script is in someone else's hand, as if an unknown entity is calling the shots. You are looking for direction from outside. This is the mindset commonly referred to as being on the 'effect side' of things. This is detrimental for your growth. This makes you feel powerless and, to some extent, limited in your choices.

Henry Ford famously said, 'Whether you think you can or think you can't, you're right.'

To succeed, you need to adopt the mindset of being on the cause side of the things.

You need to adopt the mindset that you are in control of the choices you make; you are the director calling the shots and not a mere actor acting based on instructions provided from behind the scenes. Here, the next step is taken based on your values, beliefs and subconscious patterns, which were created by you during your journey called life. You can change these patterns by making the sub-conscious conscious and taking control of the director's chair.

The clarity must come from within you because it is your authentic self knowing what is needed. When clarity is missing, it is because you have not trained yourself. That is an acquired skill but not a difficult one if you are willing to learn by having flexibility and a decision to be your own guide and perennial support.

• The trap of all-or-nothing mentality

Imagine this scenario: You purchased a brand-new car. It's shiny, eye-catching and the best model on the market. You are a proud owner, got a great deal and love taking care of the new vehicle. However, in the past you had an incident that damaged last car you owned, and you have made a resolve to be extra cautious. You have added new safety features, proximity sensors and additional cameras. All this preparation is done to assist you in keeping the resolve to drive the car safely and avoid even smallest of the damages. You go around keeping the car safe, but one fateful day, the mishap happens. You get a small scratch on the car, a really tiny one, not visible easily to the naked eye. However, for you the resolve is broken. Now you decide to just drive that car into the wall, total it out and never look at it again. Sounds weird, doesn't it? No sane person would do that.

However, when it comes to adopting new changes for improving lives, like following a healthy diet or quitting substance like sugar or smoking, if a setback occurs somehow, even for a small instance, people tend to throw all the progress in the trash, not realizing it's just a small mishap. You are allowed to fail and restart. You do not need to drop all the progress. You need to give up this all-or-nothing mentality. If something is working, small hiccups are expected; they make progress an interesting journey. Chasing a 100% record is ideal but not necessary.

The major concern I have regarding most productivity books is that they focus on how to become an ideal self. They assume if you manage your time well, you will be able to climb the mountain and perform with the energy and willpower of a monk. Wake up early, win your morning, plan your day in blocks of time, meditate to get mental clarity, do your daily journaling, be grateful, eat clean, develop a strong focus cycle, etc. All of these are noble practices that do work for many. They sound good and feel great when you start implementing them, but then after a few days, life gets in the way, and that ideal self goes missing, rarely to be seen again. A sick child, an unexpected meeting, a few bad nights' sleeps, a recession or financial stress occurs, crumbling the whole system. The ideal self is great, but it is not sustainable. Forming habits and routines does help, but there is a fine line between being consistent and being rigid. If you are not a very disciplined person, it is almost impossible to keep making these changes consistently. Behavioural flexibility is the superpower. We have to understand that being human means we will have moments of weakness; the ability to overcome drawbacks and move forward is a sign of a resilient mindset.

'A bird resting on a branch doesn't believe the branch will not break, but it trusts in the strengths of its own wings.' - Charlie Wardle

• You are unique

As I mentioned earlier, each one of us is a unique combination of values, beliefs, strengths and behavioural styles, and the same set of rules does not work all the time. What you need are solutions that are designed for your personality and lifestyle, solutions that are sustainable and implementable on a day-to-day basis. There is no magic pill that will resolve all your issues and make you a productivity superstar. In reality, there is no super-soldier serum transforming the character of Steve rogers into the superhuman Captain America, as portrayed in Marvel comics and movies. For us humans, we need to work out regularly, eat a protein-rich diet and make necessary changes in our lifestyle to gain muscles and become stronger.

Similarly, if you want to become productive and adopt efficiency in personal and professional life, the path should be simple and sustainable to achieve and maintain.

'We are all different. Don't judge, understand instead.' - Roy T. Bennett

Our standardized education system provides plenty of knowledge and guidance on how to gain basic skillset for becoming responsible individuals and learning to survive the world. And let's be honest, the system works well for a few and not so well for others. We are all unique and trying to mould our entire existence by focusing on what has worked for others will give mixed results at best.

The uniqueness of the human experience and skillset is something to celebrate. The problem occurs when we try to fit everyone in the same mould. That's why so many time management, wealth creation and mindset techniques fail the test of time.

So many books teach us to get up in the morning and try to catch the early worms. A person who gets up at 5 am and does work from 9 to 5 and goes to bed early in the night is celebrated, while someone waking up at 8 am and starting work at noon is frowned upon. This does not consider your natural rhythm, your creativity peak and ability to be at your best mental and physical state at different times of the day. Forcing a mould to fit everyone is like teaching fish to climb a tree.

Not everyone is built the same. There are variety of races in the world, and you cannot ask a marathon runner who finished a 42 km in under 3 hours to clock 10 seconds in a 100 m race, and vice versa. This is what makes us special; we tick differently, and we work well when our nature and nurture do not have a big friction. Not everyone loves the same subject, such as mathematics, and not everyone can grasp and reproduce thousands of pages worth of information. A creative individual needs freedom, not a strict timeline.

Following are some ways we are different and unique:

a. Thinking style (linear vs non-linear)

The linear thinkers love steps, processes and structure to help them make progress and get results. They love ticking off lists and details. They love planning and having a clear-cut plan to achieve things. For example, when going for a vacation or a short trip, the linear thinker is the one to come up with detailed plan and schedule with an itinerary of thigs to do and would love when things happen as per their plan.

Non-linear individuals, on the other hand, rely on creative chaos. They get flashes of insights (not understanding anything to suddenly gaining clarity). Their progress is not steady; they jump from idea to idea and get the work done as per their own timelines. For example, on a trip, non-linear thinkers would love to go with flow and decide what to do based on what is best option at that particular moment.

b. 'Through time' vs 'In time'

As discussed earlier, 'Through time' individuals are ticking clocks. You ask them to guess what the time is, and they will probably guess close to the real time. Through time individual loves keeping one eye on the deadline and are the ones who rarely miss a flight or train. Through time individual are mostly responsible for keeping everyone on schedule, and 'hurry-up or we will be late' is the sentence you will hear from them very often.

'In time' individuals tend to lose their sense of time progression and get lost in the work. They heavily rely on reminders and alarm clocks to indicate when the allocated time is up. In-time individuals, when in the zone or flow, can spend hours working on a task or an activity without even recognizing they have any deadline and often struggle to make things happen as per agreed timelines.

c. Energy peak (early riser vs. late boomers)

Early risers have their energy peak, also known as neuro golden hours, early in the morning. These individuals have a beam of energy in the early hours of the day and love to get going early. Their natural rhythm aligns with that of sun, and you will see them crashing in bed early and growing tired when they operate way past their bedtime.

The late bloomers' energy peaks later in the day. They love night life, and mornings are generally a slow affair. They take time to get started; however, they are known to end strong. The late bloomers are generally found slow and grudging in the morning and will be at their peak performance after mid-day or late in the evening.

d. Learning styles (instruction based vs. kinaesthetic)

Some individuals love being provided with instruction and help from others while learning new techniques, either through visual instructions, auditory notes or simply a logical linkage on how things operate. They learn fast in the instruction-based environment.

Kinaesthetic individuals, on the other hand, learn by doing stuff. No amount of instruction can guarantee that they have absorbed information. These individuals love when someone lets them figure out things on their own. They might take more time, but their learning is based on the experience of doing things.

e. Drivers (result vs. relationships)

Some of us are driven by task and results. Our sense of significance is attached to how our actions result in outcomes. Result-driven individuals judge others based on how the work is getting done. They will not mind causing others inconvenience if it is necessary to get the task done. They will get anxious if the results are delayed or not achieved.

Relationship-driven individuals care about how others around them are feeling and behaving, whether in a big group or small numbers. Their sense of satisfaction comes by looking at people around them and how their relationship is prospering. They will ensure others' feeling are not hurt or relationships are prioritised in most scenarios. They get uncomfortable inconveniencing others to achieve results.

f. Operating styles (disruptors vs. maintenance)

Disruptors love questioning things and the way they have been performed. They are the first to raise a concern when things get monotonous. These are change lovers and drive transitions and flourish in un-predictable circumstances. Maintenance individuals love when change is not in the horizon. They thrive in familiar environment and often resist rapid changes around them. They love familiarity and will thrive in predictable environments.

g. Our value system

The underlying operating system working behind the scenes in making choices that define our lives is our value system. We all value different things and some of them are non-negotiable. We have multiple values with their own hierarchy and our top values will drive most of our actions subconsciously. A person whose top value is freedom cannot flourish in a micromanagement environment. A rigid and strict work environment will tire them endlessly.

Our value system will act as our compass when things get murky and clarity is missing. They drive our motivation, actions and, at times, all major decisions, especially when things get complicated. Values are the reason two people in the same age group with the same skillset and same tools available at their disposal will behave differently.

Some love when their bosses or managers are involved in their work while others simply want to be left alone. Values also differ based on the context. You do not always have the same values when at work as the values you carry when you are with your family. A hyperactive and outgoing employee who loves to lead at work sometimes does not mind taking back seat when at home. Values are the core of our uniqueness and the reason why certain ways of working tick and others don't.

There are many other ways we can say everyone is unique. We are a beautiful mix of multiple styles, personality traits and behaviours, and therefore one solution might give the best result for someone while another might struggle to make it work. Leveraging this uniqueness is a must if you want to be at your most productive, and that is exactly what I am going to share through the D.O.N.E. framework. Once you align your actions with your uniqueness, you eliminate the resistance that might come from friction between your natural style of operation and adopted methods. This helps you build momentum in the right direction and sustain progress.

In analytics, the tools applied to different scenarios still work to arrive at the needed solution. They do not dictate that there is only one method to solve the issue at hand, instead simply provide the direction and enough choices to use tools with which you can create an acceptable solution.

There is a way to check if the analytical methodology is reliable in arriving at a solution. This is done through repeatability and consistency. Repeatability means that if the same framework is applied to the same set of variables and inputs (dataset and conditions), it should provide identical results, regardless of who applies it. Consistency indicates that results are similar in nature over a period of time, and even if variable changes, the methodology works to give reliable solutions.

The D.O.N.E. framework is designed to keep the parameters of repeatability and consistency in mind. The method, when applied by different people, still provides effective results. Also, when the D.O.N.E. framework is applied in a different context (apart from procrastination and overwhelm), such as goals and resolutions, the results are still effective and reliable solutions are achieved.

The first step in solving any problem is to define the problem statement carefully to capture the core. This is valid for life also; if you do not identify and define problem correctly, you might put in lot of effort but not get the correct solution. That is where the framework has its merit, because it provides structure, clarity and repeatability. It makes problems solvable not because problems get easier, but rather they get organised.

In the next chapter, we are going to discuss the D.O.N.E. framework step by step. I promise you, you are in for a simple but an exciting journey ahead. We have to keep in mind that simplification is a strength not many realise and adopt. Having complex structures and methods sounds fancy and can give some results; however, most of these results are not sustainable.

In short

1. Comparison should be done with the self, and benchmarking can be done with others.
2. Clarity comes from within you because your authentic self knows what it needs.
3. Trap of an all or nothing mentality stops you from making consistent progress. You need to adopt and embrace behavioural flexibility.
4. You are unique and D.O.N.E. framework helps you leverage your uniqueness.

CHAPTER 5

DISSOCIATE: STEP BACK, ZOOM OUT

You cannot read the label from inside the bottle. You need to step out of the mess before you can fix it. You cannot break the patterns and issues that drive procrastination and overwhelm if you do not step back to see the whole picture rationally. Dissociation does not mean completely moving out of life; it means creating enough psychological and, at times, physical distance to look at the problem without becoming part of it.

Has it ever happened to you that one of your friends or colleagues is facing a personal problem, and they are simply lost and cannot find any solution? They come to you for advice, and they start telling their problems. They may be venting out about their toxic boss, their messy relationship or their career indecision, and even before they finish the story, you have a clear understanding of what the problem is and are ready to provide them a clear, rational and well-thought-out action plan.

Compare this to when you are stuck. Suddenly it is not so simple. You overthink, you doubt, you create confusing stories and imagine the worst-case scenarios. Sometimes you just freeze and cannot imagine what needs to be done. This is the same brain that was on overdrive helping others, now simply failing to function properly, feeling like old engine operating without gasoline. This is known as Solomon's paradox—the strange phenomenon which makes solution finding for others' problems very easy and clear, while missing clarity completely while dealing with your own.

The name comes from King Solomon, ruler of Israel, known for his wisdom in solving disputes and managing his kingdom. He was great at helping others resolve their issues and provide rational suggestions for making effective decisions. He was also known to make reckless decisions in his personal life, such as taking many wives and concubines. His alliances were poor and made his kingdom weak. His personal handling of family issues made his relationships unhealthy and ultimately led to division in his reign.

This happens because when you are faced with an issue or a problem big enough to cause stress, your emotions flood and dwarf your rational thinking. You are part of the problem. Neuroscience explains this as being emotionally associated with the problem at hand. The solution is to ensure your rational thinking is not dwarfed by this emotional fog. On average, a human being faces more than 70 different emotions during a day, and all these emotions affect your decision making, sometimes in a good way and sometimes by multiplying the problems you are facing. Emotions also play a big role in determining your motivation level on a day-to-day basis. Letting emotions control your thinking is the easiest way to get lost in the problem.

Associating with the problem or a situation is a natural tendency because there are multiple hidden cognitive biases at play. They affect how you think and behave. Some of these biases are discussed below.

• Cognitive fusion (from ACT theory)

This is a sneaky trap that the brain sets up where a person becomes completely entangled in their thoughts to an extent that they are not able to separate reality from their thoughts. There is no space between what a person thinks and what is a reality. When faced with a problem, if the brain is flooded with thoughts and imaginary scenarios, it is easy to simply get lost in them. This is where overthinking and overwhelm starts creeping in. You get lost in the story your thoughts create, not realising that the monsters are not real.

• Narrow framing

This is where you end up focusing too much on small details and short-term fears instead of looking at all the variables at play to make better decisions. This results in either knee-jerk reactions or simply trying to solve the symptoms instead of concentrating on the core of the issue. Not able to get out of the bed in the morning, you blame your alarm not going off on time, or you unintentionally snoozed it because you were exhausted and needed that extra five minutes of sleep. This happens because you are not recognizing these as symptoms of not having good quality sleep for the needed number of hours. Blaming the alarm is like blaming the pen for writing in illegible language. Narrow framing does affect your work life a lot. It is easy to blame distractions and other factors for you not being able to do quality work, which puts you on the effect side of the things, as explained earlier.

• Confirmation bias

When you have existing beliefs, there is tendency to only search for evidence that confirms your beliefs. If you believe you are lazy or you cannot manage your work, you will have a tendency to get overwhelmed at the first sign of a task requiring effort and investment in terms of energy. Confirmation bias is applicable in various scenarios in life. If you don't believe me, just look at the example of 'flat earth' societies around the world. (Yes, around the world.) People will find evidence ignoring anything that challenges their belief system. The same is the case when you have internal beliefs regarding your behaviours and tendency to procrastinate. Confirmation bias sometimes hinders you from addressing the elephant in the room. Many times, you keep following patterns that do not serve you anymore just because they align with your belief system.

• Survivorship bias

This is a cognitive bias. I will explain this by using a World War II example of US bombers. The military and aviation engineers wanted to re-enforce the aeroplanes used during the battles to reduce damage and improve survivability. They looked at the data from the fighter planes coming back from the battlefield, analysed all the areas on the planes body having bullet holes and decided to reinforce these damaged areas of the fighter planes, which sounded like the most logical solution and should have improved the fighter planes survivability and battlefield performance. Abraham Wald, a mathematician, pointed out that there was a flaw in this way of thinking. The planes being analysed were shot multiple times but still made it back to the base. They survived the battlefield. They should not have been focusing on these planes but instead on the ones that could not make it back. This is called survivorship bias.

If you go to any famous tourist spot and see many restaurants and hotels having flourishing business, it is easy to assume the place must be a booming opportunity for starting a new restaurant. However, what is hidden are all those restaurant businesses that could not survive and were ultimately taken over by recent ones. Survivorship bias is something very easy to fall for. You focus on the lucrative success stories, the triumphs of how someone was able to turn their day around by using a technique that worked for them, not realising the same technique might not have worked for others. What has worked for others may not work for you, and therefore just following the others' behaviour may not guarantee success.

People who are unable to dissociate from an issue often re-experience the stress of the event later as if it's still happening—activating the same emotional and physiological responses over and over again. This can lead to chronic anxiety, fatigue and impaired decision-making—because the brain remains stuck in a loop of threat rather than a space of clarity.

Clarity comes not from rushing through and pushing further, but from stepping back far enough to see the truth beyond the noise.

Dissociating means you have to imagine or look at the problem from the point of view of a guide who is standing on the top of the mountain and can see the entire horizon. This allows you to see all the trenches, roads and dangers clearly. When it comes to personal life, you need to map things out by isolating your consciousness from your day-to-day life.

As simple way to understand dissociation is illustrated below:

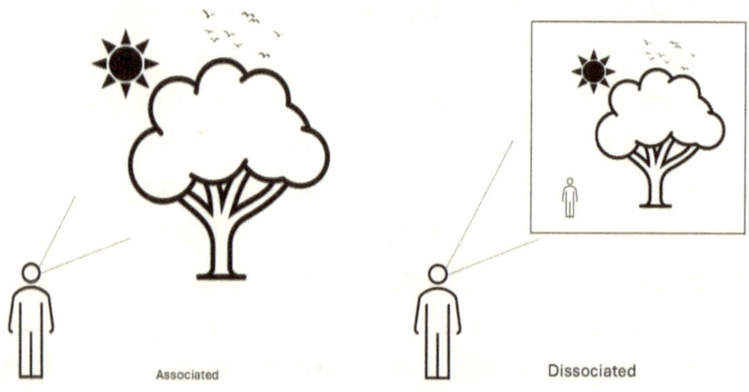

In the first picture you are seeing everything through your eyes, and you are part of the picture. You feel the temperature, air on skin, and all interactions are through your complete involvement. This is called being associated. Here you are part of the scenario, seeing through your own eyes, listening through your own ears, feeling emotions in your body and living the experience.

In the second picture, it's as if you could have stood outside the screen, looking at yourself from the third person point of view. As if it is recorded event and you are witnessing it. This is called as being dissociated. Here you can observe objectively and not feel any emotion or react to the situation. It is like witnessing a cyclone or a storm from the outside, gauging its intensity, direction, impact and movement from a distance.

This is a psychological distancing from an event which allows you to take the position of the observer instead of being a part of the scenario. Remember, when associated you behave like an actor in the movie or a scene. Things are happening to you. As I have mentioned earlier, the primary objective of the brain is survival, and any threat, big or small, can trigger a flight, fight or freeze response, blocking rational thinking. The dissociation helps you to feel safe and avoid the amygdala part of the brain from interfering.

Dissociating is a skill that can be developed with practise, and there are three simple and effective techniques that can be used to make it a habit.

1. Director, not an actor in the movie

Your life is a story in action. If you feel like an overwhelmed actor who is just performing scene after scene, then something needs to change. Unlike movie sets where the script is already written and actors simply need to perform the way it is intended, life has no lines prepared. So being an actor is stressful because you have to make every decision on the go and face the scenario and situations as they appear. With a fast-paced life, acting becomes more like reacting. The most effective way to step out of this never-ending scene is to step behind the camera, to call the shots, to set the premise and make everything fall in place by getting into the hat of a director. It may sound odd at first, but this technique comes from both cognitive behavioural practices and neuro-linguistics programming. This works wonderfully as it creates the psychological distance needed to break from the emotional entanglement of the events.

If you face a situation, if you are avoiding task, procrastinating, have emotional reactions and don't know the next step, wear the hat of the director and step back. Now watch yourself going through the moment on a screen. You're no longer the actor in the scene; you're the director watching it unfold. This allows you observe from an objective point of view, rather than focusing on what is happening and getting an emotional reaction. You focus on what needs to happen and what should be the next step to progress the story. You allow curiosity to take over instead of judgement, silencing your inner critique.

You might observe yourself sitting at your laptop or desk, blankly staring at your screen, having tense shoulders, shallow breathing, with a thousand thoughts running through your mind. You might observe yourself holding a phone and wasting time scrolling through stuff that adds no value and simply acts as a distraction from what needs to be done. This allows a new vantage point where you can see any behavioural loop at play stopping you from taking the next action, thoughts that are freezing you from getting yourself in motion and building momentum.

Remember emotions are fuelled by identification. When you are associated in the situation, any stressful situation can trigger survival mode. Dissociating helps you in creating cognitive diffusion, as it allows you to see thought as a mental event, not a command that you need to obey. You can start questioning your thoughts and any self-doubt you have. It helps you identify what is missing and what needs to occur to make things happen. It removes the fear of failure as the reactive emotions convert into insightful actions.

As a director, you can ask questions, like what is happening, what is missing, what needs to happen, what should be the next course of action, what needs to exist and what needs to change. Director can also decide to alter the mood of the situation and that the person doesn't need to perform it as a tragedy in progress.

The director can change 'why me?' to 'why not me?' and reclaim the authority of the storyline.

Let's take a practical example. Imagine you are tasked with writing a report that you are avoiding. First, the scene is performed in the associated form. You are telling yourself this is a boring task and you don't enjoy doing it at all. You fear the resultant report will not be of good quality and you will be criticised for the end result. You don't know where to start or how to structure the report outline. You find your emotions getting stronger second by second as you stare at the screen of your laptop with no progress. Suddenly, an urge comes to go and make a coffee or simply take your mobile in your hand and start scrolling to improve your mood a bit. You find yourself doing anything instead of writing the report as the clock keeps ticking but your progress bar stays still. You might devolve in self-criticism, saying you always do this, this is going to be so bad, you are lazy, etc.

Now imagine the same but from the director's chair, you see a person (you) sitting on a chair staring at a laptop screen, then you observe the person looking at a phone wasting time and not doing what needs to be done. You can see the person is struggling to come up with ideas to finish the task and not taking the necessary action. You see the hesitation, and, instead of judging, become curious as to why it is happening. The director starts asking question about how to resolve the issue and get the person moving, like changes in lighting, guidance from a colleague, a need for an outline through internet research or simply changing the environment to break the pattern. The director experiments with different takes and changes the scene rather than getting stuck and letting things play out on their own.

The dissociated director now has focused on resolving the situation instead of getting tangled in the emotional and reaction loop. This may take some practise to get used to. A simple way to dissociate is to start calling out your own name while describing the scenarios and avoid using the word 'I' as if you are describing situation of a totally different person. This will help your brain to describe the scenario with you as a character in it.

2. Note making to save mental energy

Your brain is amazing, but it is not designed to retain all the information in the world. Also, it is very easy for the brain to get lost in stories, thoughts and imaginary scenarios. At any point in time, you are bombarded with information and your brain is constantly making decisions on what to filter out and what to let through. The sub-conscious patterns keep triggering memories, thoughts and emotions all at once. This keeps your brain always busy. Science has proven that your brain is even active when you are asleep. It is a very busy organ; remember this 2% blob of fat consumes more than 20% of your daily energy intake.

When things get challenging, no wonder your already over-active brain may struggle to balance all the variables at play, making decision on the go while trying to retain all the critical information and task list saved and ready to be recalled when needed. If you have trained yourself in advanced memorisation techniques, then recalling things on the go may not be a great challenge. But if you are a normal person (normal being a technical term), then keeping all this critical information handy becomes a challenging task and requires lot more energy.

There is an easy way to help the brain by dissociating the task lists and not wasting energy on memorising stuff. Bring things out on a piece of paper or a note (voice notes also work). You need to dump down things that the brain need not keep carrying around.

Remember the beauty of the human brain lies in thinking critically and making amazing decisions, not memorising stuff.

Every now and then write down things that need to be done or simply take voice notes on the device you carry everywhere, a.k.a. your mobile phone. If you have an amazing idea, note it down. If a situation is becoming stressful, write down your thought or simply make a voice note in a dissociated manner.

Now spend a few minutes away from the problem and come back with a fresh mind and listen back or read the note written down from a third person point of view. You will realise this physical separation works wonderfully in stopping the emotional reaction and freeing the mental energy for useful stuff. This also helps in reducing mental clutter, which is discussed during the "Nudge" step of the D.O.N.E. framework in detail.

3. Define the problem using peel and reveal

The quality of question you ask yourself will ultimately determine the quality of answers you get. This is a critical step to avoid wasting energy in solving the symptoms and not the core issue. And easy way to do this is by using the peel and reveal method. It allows you to get to the core of the issue and, based on your thinking style, can be done by either using '5 WHY technique' if you are a non-linear thinker or 'pattern log recognition' if you are a linear thinker.

In the 5 WHY technique, you ask the question, 'Why it is happening?' five times in a row and use the previous answer for the next question in cascade manner. In pattern log recognition, you recreate the steps and things that happened before the issue is faced to identify if there is a common pattern at play.

Let's take a simple example: Assume that you missed your 7 am workout and are trying to identify a way to ensure you are consistent in the future. The peel and reveal will be applied as follows:

The '5 WHY' technique for non-linear thinkers

Problem: You did not work out today.

1. Why did you not work out?
Answer: Because you were tired and did not wake up on time.

2. Why were you tired and why did you not wake up on time?
Answer: Because you did not sleep well.

3. Why did you not sleep well?
Answer: Because you stayed awake till late, way past your bedtime.

4. Why you stayed awake till late, way past your bedtime?
Answer: Because you were scrolling through social media while lying in the bed.

5. Why were you scrolling through social media till late while lying in the bed?
Answer: Because you did not get time to check updates throughout the day; you were busy.

Looking at the answers we can clearly see, you did not work out because you carried mobile phone to bed. Also, you need to check the social media updates even if it is late. This gives a clear problem to solve and main reason for missing working out.

Pattern recognition log is about tracking the pattern of activities that led to the situation. In the above example of not working out, the pattern recognition log will track if a pattern exists, such as if there is a particular day of the week that you usually miss your workout, what activities and steps are taken before you face the problem and if there is a common theme every time this happens.

In the earlier example, let's apply pattern recognition: you go to bed at 10 pm. You get up at 6 am, get ready and have your morning coffee by 6:40 am, reach the gym at 6:55 am. You meet fellow members of gym class and start stretching before workout. Yesterday you did not sleep at 10 pm, instead sleeping at 11 pm and spending an extra hour checking social media updates on the phone. As a result, you did not wake up at 6 am; instead, you snoozed your alarm. So, you woke up at 6:45 am and therefore missed your workout class. Every time you are not able to get up at 6:00 am, you struggle to reach class on time. This happens when you stay awake past your bedtime. This happens on the days when you do not get time to spend on social media throughout the day and need to catch up on updates late.

Both these techniques will bring similar conclusions. However, the first technique will provide the exact reason while the second one will identify the underlying patterns.

Here the problem statement becomes 'You missed your 7 am workout class today because you stayed up late last night scrolling social media, which you could not do earlier in the day due to hectic schedule.'

So next time before you start an activity or a task, or find yourself procrastinating, use the dissociation techniques to define the problem correctly to avoid the emotional clutter and focus on actions. How to do that is discussed in the next chapter. The chapter also covers practical example on how to dissociate and **own**.

In short

1. In an associated state of mind multiple cognitive biases affect your thinking.
2. Dissociation helps you create the psychological distance needed to look at the scenario and situation logically and analytically.
3. Dissociation can be done by
   a. Acting like a director of the movie (your situation) at play.
   b. Note making to bring out the situation or problem out of your head and into the real world.
   c. Define the problem using either the "5 Why" technique if you have non-linear thinking style and the "pattern log recognition" if you have linear thinking style.

CHAPTER 6

OWN: WHAT IS YOURS TO ACT ON, AND WHAT IS NOT?

As a kid, superheroes used to fascinate me. The super strong and skilled individuals with superhuman skills fought crimes, saved the world, achieved unimaginable feats of bravery and always did what was right, even if it came at a great price. This is fantasy in general, but one theme was common: none of the superheroes were paid for their deeds, they lived average lives (if you exclude Batman who inherited money to spend). They had average jobs with average salaries. We might not have superpowers gifted to us, but we can still achieve superhuman feats. People have climbed Mount Everest to prove their strength and endurance. But hey! Do we really need to do that? We may not have a big goal or target in the vicinity of extraordinary things; however, we still tend to try to accomplish everything we can in life or whatever our job throws at us. The never-ending task lists are one of the big problems in modern life.

> *The real skill in today's world is not to get more done
> but to do what moves the needle and creates
> the impact.*

Getting bogged down by lists of things is common, especially when the list seems to be always growing. In the first step of the D.O.N.E. framework, you learned how to dissociate from the emotion and look at the problem from a neutral point of view to engage logical and analytical thinking. This helps you identify concerns and problems that need to be resolved for things to fall in place. You are responsible for making corrections and ensuring that concerns and problems are dealt with in the most appropriate manner. The secret to getting this done is the word *action*. The golden rule to remember is this:

> *All the planning in the world will take you
> nowhere if you don't take the necessary action.*

Action is the centre of all progress. Most brilliant minds can come up with a solution, but someone needs to implement the solution by taking real-world action. Having a gun with lethal ammunition will not kill the buck (sorry to the animal lovers) if you do not take aim and make the shot in the right direction. The terms 'aim' and 'right direction' are crucial here. Just shooting blindly in all directions may still hit the target, but the probability of that happening is very limited, and the possibility that you will run out of bullets before making that lucky shot is immense.

In analytical terms, you want to increase the probability of success (hitting the buck) to maximize the result (catch the prey) and reduce the losses (minimum use of ammunition).

(P.S. Probability is a mathematical term used to indicate how likely something is to happen. It indicates chance of completing an intended action successfully amongst the possible scenarios.)

So, how can we do it? This is where the step **own** of the D.O.N.E. framework becomes crucial.

Own stands for ownership of your actions.

Ownership means completely taking charge and responsibility for an action, task or problem to be solved. You need to be present 100% mentally and emotionally.

When you come across an issue, you may or may not be the correct person to deal with it. By using dissociation, you have identified the real pain point; now it's time to understand if it is your responsibility to deal with it. Many times, this energy vampire is not your problem; you inherit it from someone who is not able to deal with it. True ownership indicates you have the capability and responsibility to get the issue/task sorted, dependencies are identified, and you make sure to seek help where it is needed and delegate where it doesn't need your energy to be spent. The ownership can be with someone else.

It is not as complicated as it sounds. The simple way to do this is by asking yourselves three questions:

1.   What are the variables and what are the constants?
2.   Is there an action here that, once taken, will resolve the issue?
3.   Is the action mine to perform or not?

Let's explore why these questions work.

Question 1: What are the variables and what are the constants?

In every situation you are in, every problem you face, there are things that are going to change and things that are going to stay the way they are in the short run, or variables and constants, respectively. The key to ownership is to focus on variables as they are the factors that, when changed, can alter the outcome and make progress. Focusing on constants is simply wasting your energy and time.

A simple way to differentiate between a variable and constant is by looking at the factor and checking if it can be altered in the first place. For example, if you need to create a presentation for a client meeting, then the deadline of the presentation will be a constant, and the use of Microsoft PowerPoint to prepare can be another constant. The language used will also be a constant. The variable will be how many slides, the content of the slides, what time you allocate to prepare slides and others. All these factors can be varied and will directly affect the quality of the output.

Let's continue the example we discussed in the previous chapter, where you missed your 7 am workout and are trying to identify a way to ensure you are consistent in the future. Using peel and reveal, we defined the problem statement as 'You missed your 7 am workout class today because you stayed up late last night scrolling social media, which you could not do earlier in the day due to hectic schedule.'

What are the possible variables and constants here?

Variables (can change)
- Quality of rest
- Busy schedule affecting routine
- Tendency to snooze alarm
- Exercising in workout class only

Constants (do not change)
- Workout class at 7 am
- 30 minutes required to get ready for class
- 15 minutes of travel time to reach the class

Once the variables and constants are identified, it is essential to focus only on variables to avoid wasting energy **(variable E)** and to get actionable solutions.

Question 2: Is there an action here that, once taken, will resolve the issue?

So many day-to-day concerns that you come across are not a problem at all. I am making this bold statement because once I started asking this question through the dissociated mindset, I realised there were fewer issues in the real world than my mind used to believe. Also, it helped clearly differentiate between what is a real problem and what is just draining my emotional and mental energy.

For instance, this is easily evident in the things you are passionate about. Let's say your favourite sports team. If the team loses a key match like final of the championship, you might find yourselves drained and disappointed. Your mind starts reflecting on what could have been done differently, what factors led to loss, who is to blame and what needs to change. This becomes the discussion point for majority of your conversations with your fellow sports team lovers. I had similar experience when the Indian cricket team lost the Champions Trophy final in the 2017 to archrivals. I was so disappointed, as if I suffered a personal loss. The same happened when Australian cricket team lost an Ashes match to England during the 2023 Ashes tour.

However, until and unless we are part of decision-making body or a member of team management, all this spent energy is not going to result in anything. There is no action here which will resolve the issue as far as I am concerned.

On a day-to-day basis, you are faced with a plethora of issues you need to find solutions to as they are affecting the efficiency of your work. For example, you might be struggling to get to work on time, having too many errands to run around, having declining health (back pain is very common after a particular age), or a bad diet and lifestyle affecting health. The only way to resolve a problem is to identify what action needs to be taken to resolve the problem.

So, based on issues identified in the **dissociate** step, list all the possible actions to solve the issue. DO NOT judge any action from a practicality or implementation point of view. Trust your subconscious mind and any answer it provides. It is necessary to not judge any possible action, irrespective of how improbable it might feel at first, because it silences the inner critique and allows our subconscious to engage fully.

The following is a list from the workout example:

- Change the workout class timings (constant)
- Never miss a workout even when not going to class
- Do not allow phone or social media on bed

- Hit the bed on time everyday
- Make daily schedule less hectic
- More rest while having less sleep
- Reduce workout travel time (constant)
- Have an accountability buddy who pushes you out of bed when the snooze button is hit
- Make hitting snooze button impossible
- Sleep in the gym (all are acceptable solutions so no judgement as of now)
- Make the gym come to your place or hire a personal instructor
- Enforced time limits for social media updates

Once you have identified the list of options (without judgement) rank and shortlist actions that will bring the biggest impact when implemented (the top 3, and use the action ranked as number 1 in the list for next step). This is to ensure our variable E is focused on actions with the biggest impact.

Let's assume you identified the following action as the one with key impact.

Action: 'Hit the bed same time every night'

The solution may differ for different individuals. However, struggling with the issue and trying to survive is not beneficial in the long run because overwhelm and burnout are not far away.

Question 3: Is the action mine to perform or not?

Not all problems are your problems, and not every concern needs your attention. Remember, your energy is limited. Many times, the saviour in you just wants to resolve problems even when they are not your own. This is also called setting boundaries for yourself.

In the corporate word, getting trapped in a problem that doesn't directly belong to you is not very unusual. For an example, if you are part of the project team and get an escalation email highlighting that your team is falling behind schedule, as a responsible individual and someone who cares about the project, you might want to jump in and fix the issues at hand or at least reply to the email.

Here, take a pause and ask question: Is it mine or not?

If you are the project lead or manager, then possibly it is for you, yes.

If you are only CC'd in the email chain with no assigned task, then no.

This is very common if your friend or office colleague wants to vent out work-related frustration. You might feel giving half an hour to listen to the person venting is helping that person and you are showing empathy. However, it is going to affect your mood if you are not able to keep an objective mindset and ask if the problem is yours or not.

Having an action-focused mindset allows you to ensure your mental and emotional energy is not drained or wasted. It may also allow you to set boundaries necessary to preserve your energy. The 30 minutes you spend on a regular basis listening your bestie vent adds up soon and causes you to run out of the time you have at hand to finish your own responsibilities.

Let's continue with the example of the identified action 'Hit the bed the same time every night' for all stakeholders who are required for implementing this action. Please do not forget to involve people who will get impacted (including your spouse or partner) by those actions.

S (stakeholders): Yourself, your partner, family members, your pet.

To make the necessary changes, you will need to align expectations with the stakeholders, get agreement, support and, if possible, overcome any resistance or doubts the stakeholders might have. For example, if you have a list of tasks that need to be accomplished before hitting the bed, such as loading the dishwasher, feeding the dog, getting the trash out, a bedtime routine etc, agreeing on the timing and responsibilities of the task beforehand will increase the probability of the action being successful. For the actions involving other stakeholders, you cannot control their actions. You can only influence others by having necessary conversations, setting expectations and getting agreement.

Let's take a slightly different example involving a relationship and do the first two steps of the D.O.N.E. framework (**dissociate and own**).

Situation: Your spouse had a really bad workday, and by the time you meet, the frustration is clearly visible. On dissociating from the situation, you will realise person A (you) is faced with a scenario where person A's partner (person B) had a frustrating day at work, and they are at low energy level and not in a good mood. Person B comes and sits down on the couch and is looking at person A.

So, what are the problems statements here?

Problem 1: Frustrating day at work for person B and reasons for it.
Problem 2: Bad mood of person B because of the frustrating day person B spent at work.

Here, if you think rationally and logically. The immediate problem here for person A is how to handle the bad mood of person B only.

Once you focus on what actions that can be taken (in a dissociated manner), you will realise there are multiple options available to handle the problem at hand. It is very easy for person A to get emotionally involved and try to solve the problems person B is facing at work, but that is not the problem to solve for person A. Even with best intentions, person A can make the situation worse if they do not focus on the problem they need to solve.

What should be the action for person A to take here? What are the options available for person A?

Person A should encourage person B to share their frustration over a nice drink (tea/coffee/wine).

Or

Person A should take steps to create a nice atmosphere for person B to relax and overcome a frustrating day in a way that person B appreciates.

Or

Assume that person B is an adult and can handle problems themselves. Person A avoids person B till person B sorts out the problem.

Or

Person A jokes around and distract person B, helping person B to move on.

Or

Person A should keep staring at person B, till the time person B stops looking at person A.

Whatever is the action taken, the action will be focused on self and directed at solving the main problem that is actually yours.

'Don't carry what was never yours to lift.'

There is also a key difference between ownership of task and prioritisation of task: Prioritisation is listing the tasks while ownership is about identifying tasks that should be handled by you or not. It's binary, not having levels. A task that is high priority may sometimes need no action from you, rather for you to simply inform the responsible individual to take necessary action.

A key challenge in ownership is perfectionism. Perfectionism is a major hurdle if not an enemy to ownership. Many people justify perfectionism as taking full responsibility of task, which sound like ownership, but it is not. Perfectionism is not about responsibility; it is about control. Many people face it when they have perfectionism tendencies, everything needs to be done in certain way and to a specific standard. Correcting someone else's slides, delaying a decision as you want to be thorough and polished, not being able to delegate, attaching self-worth to the task outcome are all signs of perfectionism. Ownership, on the other hand, focuses on eliminating work that is not actionable, maximising options at hand, and ensuring the actions you take are in the right direction. It is about energy and focus, not controlling the outcome.

Remember when you focus on actions and take ownership of a problem and task, you are making progress in the right direction. You are not trying to do everything under the sun, just trying to identify what actually moves the needle. Focus on action, not reaction. Ask yourself these questions:

1. *Will the action here, once taken, resolve the issue?*
2. *What are the variables and constants here?*
3. *Is the action mine to perform or not?*

In short

1. You need to increase probability of success for your goals by owning only high impact actions.
2. Identify the key variables and constants in the short run. Focus only on the variables, not the constants.
3. Focus your energy on actions that are under your control by setting boundaries and aligning expectations with key stakeholders.

CHAPTER 7

NUDGE: HELP THE FUTURE YOU!

The human brain is amazing. It can store millions of bits of information, become skilled at any skill known to mankind, push us to achieve amazing deeds and everything else while also having this silly habit of creating doubts and uncontrollable non-supportive emotions that make us go blank and freeze when it matters the most. Hours and hours of practice cannot guarantee you will perform well on the final stage if you are not used to and prepared for how your emotions and thoughts can betray you, something we label as 'self-doubt'. Your brain cannot differentiate between what is real and what is imaginary. Many times, these imaginary demons can freeze you in the path of making progress and doing what needs to be done. Sometimes even a small misstep will ring alarms as if catastrophe has hit and everything is doomed, and you end up giving up what you were excited to do.

You need to ensure these hurdles of self-doubt and possible missteps are tackled quickly. That your start is smooth and frictionless and once you get going, you have a momentum that sets you up to make progress consistently. This is done by ensuring you have support that nudges you to move forward and gets you going.

Recall the last time you wanted to do something. For example, writing a book, playing guitar, taking culinary classes, learning to ride a horse or going for adventure sports. Let's take an example of learning the guitar. If you decide you need to learn the guitar, you cannot start it right away; you need to buy the guitar first. You also need to identify where you are going to learn the basics like tuning a guitar (you will need a tuner), figure out where you will practise it, learn the chords (taught by a teacher or YouTube channel), etc. When all this is done, then you will take the first step. So, if you need to start learning guitar tomorrow, to help your future self in getting started, you will need to act today by preparing all that needs to be prepared.

> *You need to help your future self!*

Because if you get ready (mentally) to start but find that one piece is missing, whatever it may be, you are likely to face resistance and stop progress.

So why does this happen?

• Path of least resistance

The human brain loves familiarity. It is an amazing organ but also a lazy one. When you are about to start a new task, something you know is going to take effort, your brain starts raising alarms as if it is the end of the world. If you have an option, the brain will pick the option that requires the least amount of energy. Brain will avoid resistance and push back when it feels that something is difficult. Removing this resistance in advance by taking necessary steps of preparation tricks the brain into thinking this is easy and doesn't need much effort for getting started. For example, if you have to prepare a meal and it requires you to start chopping vegetables, the brain may feel it is too much. But if the vegetables are already chopped in the refrigerator, there is a pan on the stove and all you need is to start the burner and start cooking, the brain feels that the task is already started and it may as well finish it. Removing initial resistance is the easiest way to get things done. The initial resistance doesn't come from lack of drive but lack of action.

• Decision fatigue

Making decisions is one of the most challenging tasks for the brain because it also must spend energy in weighing pros and cons of each decision. An average person can only make limited number of quality decisions in a day, and if you plan ahead, the number of decisions can be reduced. Let's say you have a meeting tomorrow. Choosing a dress in advance (when fear of last-minute rush is missing and the brain is not in panic mode), getting footwear ready and preparing your bag with accessories like keys will help you to get going without making any decisions because they were already made for you previous day. It removes the chances of you missing critical things while you are running against the clock.

• Resting inertia

Resting inertia, in technical terms, is defined as the tendency of an object to stay at rest until it is acted upon by an external force. Objects take the most effort and energy in getting started, and the pushback is the strongest at this stage. If you really want to move ahead, you need to support yourself for that moment when you are trying to push an object at rest. This is easily visible when you are sitting on the sofa, watching TV or a streaming service and need to do dishes. Nothing is stopping you from getting up and get going, but there is an unhinged force keeping you grounded on that cosy couch, ultimately causing procrastination.

• You cannot predict your future emotional state

Last-minute panic, internal resistance and self-doubt are not uncommon. Emotions can come up at any time. They are triggered by external stimuli, which you may or may not be aware of. One of my personal pet peeves is someone littering in public transport places (a disposed cup or soda can on a train seat just triggers me), and if I am not able to regulate my emotional state there, irritation and anger are simply waiting to jump in to take over my brain. This is a distraction and can derail the momentum I have built in doing what I was doing.

• Survival mode

The amygdala, a.k.a. reptilian brain, is the part of the brain responsible for keeping us safe to a certain extent in case of imminent danger. An evolutionary gift which kept the human species safe from all the dangers, such as sabre-toothed tigers and other predators, when hunting and gathering were our occupations. The human species has evolved to become agrarian, then industrial and now an information-driven society; you do not have an apex predator scanning you before attack when you order food online anymore. The amygdala is still needed to save us from car accidents, or taking silly risks, but it cannot differentiate between imaginary fears and fears originating from real world entities. Fear of speaking in public has the same emotional response that of getting hit by a bullet train head on (flight, fight or freeze response). Without preparing for this, there is no way you can regulate your emotions and help your future self.

Do you know when faced with an imminent danger, there is a phenomenon known as amygdala hijack? For six seconds, your brain shuts down all logical and rational thinking as if an override has been added. During this interval, the amygdala floods your entire system with panic and fear, triggering the flight or fight response. This causes you to freeze, snap or simply panic. This is the brain's automatic response to danger.

When you are living in survival mode, your pre-frontal cortex struggles to overcome the flood of emotional overdose in your system, ultimately leading to exhaustion and overwhelm. To avoid it, you need to train yourself to operate not from the survival mode, instead adopting growth mode where you are in charge and engaging your logical thinking.

Help Your Future Self

> *'Do something today that your future self will thank you for.' - Sean Patrick Flanery*

What I mean by saying help your future self is to create a plan in order to prioritize the objective and overcome inertia, to ensure that when the need arrives you are not letting your emotions, such as fear, take over your rational thinking, removing any physical barrier which might stop the momentum you have built. It means eliminating what might become an obstacle both mentally and physically. This is internally driven, slightly different from the preparations you do, as the locus is internal. You are looking from your perspective, and priority is on both material and emotional things.

How do you achieve this?

1. Do the journey in the mind first

Closing the eyes and imagining how things will pan out (remember the brain cannot differentiate between what's real and what's imaginary) will trigger the same emotional response today. You need to do it three times (best case, worst case and most likely scenario) for any upcoming event or activity. Let's take an example of you preparing for an upcoming presentation to the management for a new product launch. You have taken all the necessary information needed, created slides and done proof readings. On the day of the presentation the following two scenarios can occur:

Scenario A:

You come to the meeting room just in time, and everyone is already there. You start setting up the presentation and realize the projector is not working. You need to restart it, and that takes three to five minutes. Once the projector starts, the screen is slightly tilted and the colours are off, but there is no time to correct it as the meeting has already started, and you are ready to start presenting. You look around and because of the delay, some of the members of the team have already started chatting amongst themselves, some are typing on laptops, and mobiles screens are also being stared at. You now need to bring attention back to the room, and it takes few more seconds before everyone is looking at you. You thank everyone for their patience and start presenting. And even before you complete the first slide, a few questions start floating around. You start answering those questions, and before you know it the first slide itself has taken more than 15 minutes as more doubts keep coming up. This continues, and even before you have completed half the presentation, the meeting time is over. Some members need to leave, and you decide to send them the slides separately plus book time for follow-up meetings. Your boss doesn't look happy, and that sinking feeling of imminent failure creeps in.

Scenario B:

You arrive ten minutes early to the meeting and check the projector. It has some issues which you quickly sort out. As everyone arrives in the meeting, you greet all the attendees, and as they settle down you are ready with a big smile, all set to go. In the first 30 seconds, you hand everyone a printed handout of the presentation with a summary and a few FAQs you expect to come during the discussion, which you mention will answer most questions. You also suggest that questions and answers have allocated time at the end.

You go through all the presentation slides with full confidence, and before you know it, it's time for Q&A. There are some tricky questions, but you answer them to the best of your ability and also get support from your seniors and boss to tackle some challenging ones, and the meeting is over before stipulated time. Your boss is happy with you for the great presentation, and you leave the room beaming with confidence.

Both of these scenarios were imaginary. However, while reading them you might have observed that a few emotions do creep in. How things will pan out in reality (most likely scenario) can be slightly different, but it will be somewhere in the vicinity of both above mentioned scenes. There can also be a fire alarm right in the middle of the presentation and you will need to evacuate the room (external contingency), which will require evasive action as physical safety is always a priority. But by providing printed handouts, at least you have ensured people are given information that they need from the meeting.

By evaluating bad scenarios and good ones, you have already allowed your brain to experience the emotional reactions that might come up later. This helps eliminate the fear of the unknown, helping your future self. This also allows you to prepare the physical environment and mitigate risks.

If we continue the example in the previous chapter where the identified action through first two steps (Dissociate and Own) was "Hit the bed the same time every night," here are the possible scenarios:

Best case scenario: You finish all the pending tasks for the day, follow the bedtime routine, switch off the light, and get in the bed. The room temperature is ideal, and the smell of fresh, warm bedsheet gives a cosy warm feeling. There is silence and a pleasant atmosphere. You fall asleep quickly and get good rest.

Worst case scenario: You have many tasks remaining and decide to keep them pending for the next day. You had to drink many cups of coffee throughout the day to keep your concentration level up. You lose the track of time and work past your decided bedtime. When the realisation hits, you start the bedtime routine but get an urgent call. In the room, the temperature is not ideal (too cold or too hot) and air conditioner is not available. The bed is not well made, so you have to prepare the bed, there are no fresh bed sheets, and the bed frame shows signs of damage. As you get in to bed, the neighbour's dog starts barking loudly and will not shut up. Then you lie down in the bed and stay awake, staring at the ceiling. Boredom takes over, and you scroll social media, wasting time. Because of late evening coffee, you keep waking up at night multiple times and do not get quality sleep.

Most likely scenario: You finish most tasks that needed to be completed today, leaving a few tasks that could be done tomorrow without any major impact. There is an alarm reminding you to start the bedtime routine. During the routine, there is possible distraction (a call or social media update) which you quickly attend to within five minutes. As you go in the bedroom, the room temperature is not ideal but manageable through a minor altercation with the AC, fan or blanket. The bed sheets are normal and acceptable, and the bed is ready and just needs a small patting. As you lie down, you reflect on the day, take four or five minutes to fall asleep. You get up once in the night, but the sleep quality is decent and uninterrupted.

This journey done in the brain clearly indicates what needs to happen for things to flow smoothly for achieving the target action. It also allows you to prepare and mitigate the possible risks that may arise.

2. Focus on the value of your action

Things that have a sense of urgency become priority by default and take the most attention. Survival is always the priority. The focus automatically shifts to the urgency in the short run that needs to be dealt with, leaving behind the tasks that can have bigger impact in the long run. This leads to a never-ending cycle of moving from one task to another, one crisis to another, not realising all these small things add up to create stress and fatigue, which, if not dealt with, cause overwhelm. We need to prioritize the things that matter, the things that will affect our greater objective. Many of these so-called crises get averted by themselves. All you need to learn is to say 'wait'. The majority of the crises are energy vampires and do not require your actual attention. Ask a simple question to identify if the urgency is worth looking at:

'What value is my action going to add?'

Remember your attention and action are both critical resources, and we need to save and manage the use of these resources. If the action you are going to do is not adding value, you are wasting energy.

The simple way to identify this is by asking, 'Will my future self be content' with the result? Does it have enough impact to require me spending my energy on it? Is it really that important?

I will take an example of my toddler struggling to put on his shoes while going to daycare. We might be late if my toddler struggles for the next five minutes, or the kid might throw a tantrum and in an upset mood make the journey to daycare even worse. Sounds urgent, prompting me to just go ahead and tie his shoes myself. But then realize this: This issue might keep repeating in the future, and always giving it attention will not make my future self content. Instead, I should channel my energy into guiding or letting my toddler figure out how to wear his own shoes. This will save me hours in the future, and therefore a few minutes of investment now is worth it. My action should not focus on shoes but the toddler's ability to deal with this himself. Sometimes I just need to let him struggle because self-learning is the easiest way to remember things. The choice of whether to act or not is yours. Focus on how it impacts your future self.

3. Adopt 'ready to go'

You need to be ready to go into action at any time. If you need to go to the office, having your bag ready with a laptop, charger, office access pass and a water bottle at a fixed place where you can simply pick up and leave the door means being office ready. Car keys and house keys can also be part of this. If you are traveling overseas, having your passport and visa documents already packed and available in your handbag will avoid a last-minute struggle to check the bag and frantic search. Having a cab pre-booked to pick you up a couple of hours in advance is a blessing.

The idea here is if there is an upcoming action that needs preparation, minimize the effort that you need closer to the occurrence of the event. This will not only save time but also ensure you are in a good mindset, focusing on what matters and not wasting energy on things that require relying on your memory at the last minute or having the concern that you might forget something. When you prioritize your future wellbeing, almost acting like an assistant to your future self, you minimize the energy that is otherwise wasted by Future you. You are eliminating friction and resting inertia.

Keeping a water bottle and a snack (healthy in nature, preferably) near your office table (while in the office or working from home) will stop future you in wasting time travelling to the kitchen or cafeteria (depending on where you are working from) and grabbing whatever you find at the last minute (usually an unhealthy snack). When you prioritize your future self, you stop unnecessary action that would have otherwise occurred.

For the identified action of 'Hit the bed at the same time every night', the following are needed to adopt the 'ready to go' mindset:

- Keeping the bed prepared
- Not having coffee in the late evening
- Keeping late night calls or social media updates limited to less than five minutes (a reminder alarm can be used here)
- Having noise-cancelling earplugs and sleep mask handy
- Setting an alarm to remind you of bedtime routine start time

You might think this can take so much effort and time. In reality, by prioritizing your future self and investing energy and time now, you are making things easier for your future self and saving time. I used to be late in the traffic of Mumbai, where every minute delay multiplied and got me even more late. When I started adopting an office-ready mindset, the time I left for my workplace became consistent and I was rarely late.

You can start small by focusing on only one thing at a time. You don't need to get everything started all at once. Focus on one major thing that drains your energy the most. It can be as simple as keeping a laptop and charger in the bag and keeping the car/house keys ready by the door every day. Start small and build the momentum. Sustainable changes take time to stick.

You might also feel that other stakeholders and people involved can ruin it; you can't do it alone. This is where the ownership comes in handy. Focus on what you can control. If it is not actionable, then it is not worth thinking about.

You might also think your daily schedule keeps changing and you do not have certainty about what to expect the next day; you can be working from home some days and traveling some days. Keeping laptop bags ready to go near your home office in its allocated space will have the same impact. It will also signal your brain to properly switch off from work at the end of every day as you have created a physical anchor, an action that makes transitioning from work to home easy. I prefer to shut down my laptop every day and keep it packed away.

The following are the three simple things that you can start doing today which will make your future self's life easier and smoother:

1. Identify the tasks that take the most energy and list one action that will make it easy for you.

Do that action first or simply give it to someone else who is willing to do it. Involve the stakeholders and seek help if the task or action is very difficult for you. You can use technology as well. For example, in order to not waste time scrolling social media in bed, you can set an alarm and activate night mode on your mobile phone at the designated time in the night. You can also seek help from your partner and simply hand over your mobile phone to them till morning.

2. Design a reward system.

There are two types of rewards:

    a. Positive reward that encourages good behaviour
    b. Negative reward that punishes bad behaviour

Both positive and negative rewards play a very crucial role in framing behaviours. Always combine the two and see what works for you. You might have heard regarding classic carrot-and-stick analogy. Some of us are motivated by the promise of positive gain at the end, such as rewards, praise, pleasure and recognition. Others find fear of punishment or a desire to avoid pain as their driving force, e.g. fear of failure, judgement, loss or punishment. Neither of these is inherently better or worse; what matters here is to understand what makes you move and get going and which one freezes you, leading to procrastination and overwhelm.

3. Be kind to yourself and thank your past self.

We all have those days where things simply don't work out. In spite of all the effort we put in, things fail. This is the time we need to avoid the all-or-nothing mentality. A small failure should not cause you to throw away the system you created. It is like throwing your brand-new dress in the dumpster when you get a small stain on it. If you fail, start again. Do not throw away something that has been helpful for your future self. Keep helping and taking small steps to make your future self thank you.

Also, when you see the benefits, thank your past self for being so considerate and making your life easy. Be grateful for all the support and help.

Nudging works well in getting you to start supporting your future self. However, there are still a few changes you can make to your lifestyle to make it happen effortlessly. Before we move on to the **E: Elevate** step in the D.O.N.E. framework, the next chapter will discuss how to make nudging easier by eliminating friction and ensuring there are no energy vampires limiting your energy levels. The fast-paced life often leaves lots of residue and clutter that sometimes becomes part of your being. In the next chapter, we will identify some of this clutter and learn how to eliminate it to make progress even better and procrastination almost non-existent.

In short

1. Help your future self by identifying all the potential hurdles in getting started.
    a. Do the journey in the mind first by imagining best case, worst case and most likely case scenario.
    b. Ensure your action is adding value and it makes your future self content.
    c. Always be ready to go by minimizing effort closer to the event.
    d. Design a reward system.
    e. Be kind to yourself.

CHAPTER 8

THE ELIMINATION FILTER: ELIMINATE TO ACCELERATE

'Less is more' is a phrase that is commonly used to declutter surroundings and embrace minimal living. The core idea is to ensure you do not have many things that serve minimal or no purpose in your life and are there just because you thought you needed them, while in reality they are not necessary in the first place. When you love certain things, getting rid of them is very difficult. They are not purchased with the intention that they are useless and are going to clutter your life; you buy them because they have a certain appeal which is trying to satisfy one of your wants or needs (the difference is explained later). The decision to purchase that stuff was for a purpose and a good reason. Sometimes that decision doesn't serve you, and those objects become a hindrance to cleanliness and space in your surroundings.

Similarly, you are faced with so many decisions in your day-to-day life that feel correct while you are making them. They satisfy a want or a need. We all know that scrolling social media (for instance, TikTok, Instagram or YouTube) may result in wasting your time, but you make that decision because it serves a purpose like creating an escape from boredom, connecting with people you admire or searching for an answer that is missing in your knowledge base. The decision feels correct at that moment, but when you reflect on it, it feels wasteful and like it could have been avoided. Hindsight is always 20/20. 'I should have done this and not that' is easy to say during reflection, not while you are in the centre of the decision making. That is why dissociation is so critical while making decisions.

There is another benefit of hindsight: you can plan to eliminate incorrect decisions from your life, just like removing unnecessary purchases from your surroundings to declutter. This is where elimination is crucial.

By eliminating, I meant you make the decision to remove actions that do not serve the purpose they are intended for.

*'The ability to simplify means to eliminate
the unnecessary so that the necessary may speak.'
- Hans Hofman*

Elimination is good because it allows you to focus your effort and energy on one thing at a time. For instance, in our family 'What should be made for dinner?' was one of the most dreaded questions, especially during COVID lockdowns. Most of the shopping was done online, and we usually had enough ingredients at home to make different meals. For the first few days this was fun because we enjoyed a variety of dishes, having enough time at hand and nothing else to do. But soon the same question led to tiny argument about who should make that decision on a particular day. We even started keeping score like 'I decided yesterday, now it's your turn'. Even the quality of decisions was debated a lot with arguments such as 'You always choose the same dish, think of something else', or 'I don't like that dish, making it will take lot of time, change the choice'.

As the restrictions eased up and normality returned, the situation got worse. We could still order ingredients through online shopping, but we didn't have enough energy left at the end of the day and just wanted to have a meal and relax. That extra decision of what we should eat when we were already low on energy added frustration and, at times, felt overwhelming, leading to further arguments, with no one willing to make the choice because it required consideration and identification of which dishes could be prepared and enjoyed. This is just a simple example, but you can find yourself in similar scenarios while holiday planning, buying gifts, choosing clothes etc., anything that requires making a choice after weighing pros and cons.

Many get overwhelmed just trying to do what needs to be done daily. The household chores become too much, the office (even on a low-stress workday) feels overwhelming, you run out of time and mostly out of energy.

Why does this happen?

• Decision fatigue

It is a cognitive phenomenon that occurs because of the limited capacity of brain in making decisions every day. Every decision you make consumes energy, irrespective of how big or trivial it is. When you are making decisions every minute of your day, you are constantly depleting your energy reserve. Even small amounts of thinking trigger the pre-frontal cortex region of your brain, and too many decisions will tire you. When you allow your life to become a series of decisions, you are ensuring your brain is fried at the end of the day (figuratively). Every choice you make, whether for growth, survival or just existence, needs an investment of energy.

And if you are keen on making amazing decision every time, the considerations and criteria make decision making even more energy consuming.

• High need for variety

As discussed in Chapter 4, we are all individuals with different needs, and each of these needs is part of a spectrum. You will either be someone requires high degree of variety in life or somebody who is keen on maintaining familiarity. This is evident in multiple aspects of your life such as travel, choice of clothes, footwear, career and even the choices of entertainment. Many love to watch the same movie or series over and over while others will keep searching for what's new in the catalogue. When you have individuals clashing in their need for variety, it is but natural for friction to emerge.

The catch here is that if you have a high need for variety, the number of decisions you make will grow, requiring a lot of energy. For instance, if you have a wardrobe with the entire spectrum of colours and styles, decision fatigue is more common as a lot of energy is spent in making the decision of what to wear on a particular day. It is not wrong to have a high need for variety; however, it does come with a cost, and you may need to put in some conscious effort to limit the number of decisions you have to make.

• Designed procrastination for presumed failure

I will elaborate on this with an example of one of my old roommates and his morning routine. Let's call him Rick. Whenever Rick had to get up at 4 am to catch an early flight, he would set up four alarms: the first at 3:30 am, the second 3:40 am, the third one at 3:50 am and the final at 4 am. When I confronted Rick and told him that this bothered me and asked for his reasons, the answer was simple. Rick believed he could not get up the first time the alarm went off; he needed multiple chances of waking up, each alarm a warning and preparation to wake up on time.

This was his strategy to get up because Rick has presumed his failure in acknowledging the alarm at 4 am. He needs those three warnings before the most crucial alarm. This is planned procrastination.

The example might look weird, but there is snooze button with every alarm, and almost all of us are guilty of pressing it for that extra five minutes of sleep. The design of snooze is to allow us to delay the action of getting out of bed.

For some, it becomes a go-to strategy. They tend to add additional steps to things that you can just get started at and improve the chances of your success, not realising all these additional steps actually consume energy at each instance. This results in over-planning, focusing more on results and not on action.

• Focusing on 'want' instead of 'need'

As a human, you have some basic needs for survival. These include nourishment, hydration, clothing, shelter, social support, breathable air, rest and reproduction. Maslow's hierarchy of needs has highlighted this necessary for survival. Needs are simple and in their basic form.

Let's take example of hydration. You have necessity to stay hydrated for your physical survival. Your body composition has almost 69% water. Water is found freely in nature and is plenty enough to give us the necessary hydration. However, you go to any supermarket and you have options of energy drinks, carbonated soda, a variety of mineral waters, caffeinated drinks, fruit juices, etc. competing to get your attention. Each with a variety of selling points proving you should spend your money and focus on them to fulfil your need for hydration. Most of these choices did not exist few centuries back, and still the human race survived and even flourished. So why so many options?

Your needs are limited; your wants are unlimited.

The entire marketing industry targets your wants: to feel special, to be unique, to stand out, to have many choices, to get results quickly, to be faster and to become better. You struggle to choose among the options because these artificial notions of variety make you forget your core needs. It is easy to get overwhelmed with choices. For instance, if you want to travel between two cities, you only need to worry about three things: how much time you are willing to spend on travel (affects variable T), how much energy will it take to go from point A to point B (affects variable E) and the amount of money you can afford to spend (affects variable R). If you want to maximize variable E and T (reduce the time and energy spent on travel), you'll likely need to spend more money to book a flight. If you are willing to spend more time and energy, then the option changes to car, and when you don't want to spend energy and are willing to spend time but not money, public transport becomes the go-to option. When you think about the fundamental variables at play and focus on the core need (travelling between point A to point B), the choice becomes simple.

It is easy to get overwhelmed if you get distracted by whether to fly economy or the first class (incremental comfort is a want), or whether to drive a basic car or a luxurious brand. Deciding between wants takes lot more from variable E and variable T and you willingly spend it without even realising that you have been tricked into spending unnecessary energy on decision making.

Needs are the basics and are core in nature while wants are simply layers or emotional desires added on top. Not focusing on necessity is an easy way to get lost and feel overwhelmed when the choices feel unlimited.

> *'Only about 20% of the things you buy are based on actual need. The other 80% are driven by emotional wants shaped by marketing.'*

This was the finding in one of the research projects conducted by Harvard professor Gerald Zaltman, highlighting that almost all (~80%) of purchasing decisions are made subconsciously, driven by emotions, identity and social validation—not logic or core need.

Now that you have understood that life is cluttered with complexity, how do you adopt simplicity, make things more manageable and avoid overwhelm? The answer is the elimination factor, the ability to remove and detach from the unnecessary.

Elimination is about ensuring you keep your choices focused, like a beam of light, and not scattered. Elimination reduces cognitive overload by preserving your brain's most limited and valuable resource: attention. The human brain is a prediction machine, constantly filtering, prioritizing and deciding among inputs. Elimination is about getting rid of the noise, decluttering the thought process and reducing the cognitive load that happens because of decision fatigue, unlimited wants and focusing on outcome instead of action.

There are simple ways you can adopt the elimination factor in your lives:

Step 1. Identify the clutter

If you can identify it, you can correct it. When you dissociate and look at things objectively, you need to ask yourself, 'What is the purpose (core need) of the activity or thing you are spending your energy on?" The clutter can be of multiple types such as the following:

a. Physical clutter:

This one is typically easy to spot, though at times it can be difficult to recognise. If you are living in a household with multiple gadgets, you might find a drawer with old earphones, extension cords, cables and accessories that were stored for future use but haven't been touched for years, occupying unnecessary space. Clothes that haven't been tried for years and are either saved for a special occasion or are simply there due to emotional attachment (even though they are never used).

I personally struggled with painting and drawing stationary from the days when my wife and I used to paint and sketch. I also struggled with old sporting gadgets and instruments purchased when available on an awesome deal and never used. A simple rule can be used here to distinguish the clutter from useful stuff: If a thing hasn't been used in last one year and it exists only for some future scenario that will not occur in the next six months, it is clutter. You need to get rid of it by giving it away to charity, re-selling, recycling or chucking it in the waste bin.

b. Psychological clutter:

These are not easy to spot, and you might need some guidance and support to identify it. Psychological clutter appears generally in the form of rules, beliefs and patterns that have been part of your day-to-day life that do not serve you anymore. For instance, when I was a kid living in a village, it was a rule that all outdoor physical activities, such as playing sports, exercising or travelling should happen during daytime and end before sunset. It was mandatory to be back indoors before night fell. The village had limited street lighting, and being close to farms in the secluded region, it was logical as at nights wild animals, street dogs and anti-social elements used to be a safety hazard. Being at home before sunset ensured we were safe from danger. When I moved to a city, I was still following that rule without consciously thinking, and it did interrupt my daily schedule. Whenever I ended up working late hours in the office, I would skip exercise that day as I was not supposed to exercise after sunset. This happened quite regularly, and it did affect my health and lifestyle in general.

When I became aware that this rule was still at play (subconsciously) and it was not serving me anymore, I had to make a conscious effort to change it. It took some time adjusting and getting those late evening workouts. Many of you are guilty of following outdated rules without even realising. For example, needing that morning coffee even after having good night sleep, smoking after lunch, eating sweets after a meal or having a drink on Friday evening. If these rules still serve you, then it is ok to continue. But a person struggling financially may need to re-evaluate spending money on drinks before every weekend in a pub when the same drink is a lot cheaper to buy from a liquor store to be enjoyed at home. Eliminating drinking altogether, till finances are back on track, is even better. The excuse that it is socialising activity and, therefore, going to the pub for a drink is a good habit indicates a lack of clarity in defining the problem.

c. Social clutter:

This one is a tough one to get rid of, as it is generally camouflaged in years and years of conditioning and beliefs systems. Social clutter means identifying those relationships that are detrimental to your progress and well-being. These are relationships that drain your mental and emotional energy and have limited benefits.

Let's be honest, social relationships are one of the core needs. However, not all relationships are healthy. For instance, the relationship with that work colleague who loves to gossip near the water cooler about other colleagues, the relative whose presence makes every family function feels like a battlefield with constant criticism and fault finding, nosey neighbours who keep an eye on your every movement but keep their distance when you need support, a friend whose presence only happens during fun times, but crisis make them vanish into thin air.

I was raised in a culture where social approval was key for judging every action, and my parents made sure we were always reminded of it when making any decision. 'What will people say?' was a hypothetical question raised almost every time we did something new or creative. Blending into the societal norm was more important than being authentic; having others approval was more critical than identifying personal passion and individual identity. This impacted every crucial decision, including career (should make them feel proud), marriage (arranged marriage was good, love marriage was bad), social dynamics (always respect the elder, even when that elder was epitome of toxic behaviour) and others. Breaking this social conditioning is a tough pill to swallow, especially when you are part of a society where standing out is seen as a sin and being successful is considered breaking the norm, as it distances some people and hinders social approval.

These social norms and rules originated in the earlier stages when human society was not so interconnected. We used to live in tribes, and standing out was a sure way of becoming target of the rival clans. It was like a zebra having black and white stripes to blend in with the others in its herd. It made it difficult for predators to target a single zebra. Similarly, getting social approval and blending within societal norms ensured people survived together. Social expectations became a binding factor for the stability and progress of society. It was a by-product of survival mindset. In war-torn societies or situations of abject poverty, the survival mindset is still valid and prominent. However, if you have reached a certain level in life where survival is not the core of existence, these bits of social clutter in the form of expectation, norms and rules create a hindrance to progress and drain energy by limiting options and cluttering your thought process.

Remember, in order to eliminate this clutter, there are only two options:

- Change your physical surroundings to limit interaction.
- Identify the rules and get rid of the guilt and emotional baggage of these expectations.

The first option is relatively easier if you have flexibility of movement. The second one requires more deep thinking and having firm belief in your own abilities. This needs adoption of authenticity and self-love as a core belief. Once this is done, the external criticism (not feedback) will sound like mere words and will not invoke any emotional response within you. This can be done by using emotional dissociation (taking an objective lens on every word being shared and identifying if there is any action involved, the **own** step of the framework). If you do not have any actions you need to take, you do not need to own it.

d. Mental clutter:

If your brain feels like a browser with 50 tabs open simultaneously, with music playing in the background and everything feeling slow and tiresome, you are not alone. Overstimulation, multitasking and having a tendency to jump from one task to another is not uncommon. Identifying this mental clutter is the first step in making progress. Clarity makes it easy to identify what is serving you and what needs to be eliminated. Having a cluttered mind will make you tired faster than running a 10K within an hour. It is a first sign that overwhelm and procrastination are just a step away. However, this one is easier to identify and simpler to correct.

There are multiple techniques available to get rid of mental clutter. We have discussed dissociating to gain clarity. Writing down stuff on either a piece of paper or a notepad on your laptop stops the brain from jumping tabs. This years-old technique works like a wonder as it allows you to separate reality from the imaginary.

I had a fellow international student during my MBA days who was feeling frustrated. During a break, she was talking about how many things were happening, and she simply could not concentrate on the upcoming presentation. When I asked her what those things were, the answer felt like blabbering mess with many concerns and deadlines. It included a visit to embassy, a pending bank transaction, an overdue project report, an upcoming exam and personal stuff, all coming up in the same sentence. I recommended that she write down everything and just put the date next to each activity so that I could make sense of it, or at least identify when she could start working on the project. The change in her facial expression and the relief she felt was so clear, as if this simple act of writing it down made her mind release the weight it had been holding for so long. She realised her embassy appointment was not until the next week, the pending bank transaction didn't require action from her, the overdue project would just need couple of hours and all the other personal stuff was more imaginary and also didn't need any action from her.

Mental clutter is a clear sign that you are allowing emotions to take over and not using your logical thinking. It also indicates you are not focusing on actions needed and instead factors beyond your influence. The **dissociate** and **own** steps in the framework are crucial to eliminate this mental clutter and make friends with clarity.

e. Temporary clutter:

These are bits of situational clutter that appear from time to time and may not need long term consideration. However, this clutter does tend to affect your efficiency and still needs to be identified. It is like sitting in a library and a bunch of school-going teenagers decide to sit behind you and discuss their upcoming examination. Out of nowhere, the discussion becomes noisy enough to distract everyone, including you. Even though those teenagers are generally well-behaved and follow the library rules to maintain peace and use a gentle voice, they forget to follow the norms, and a simple interception from someone asking them politely to keep the noise down can resolve this issue. You are also faced with plenty of short-term clutter in your life and need to recognize that these clutters are temporary and need simple actions.

Step 2: Decide the 'target state'

This step is applicable for every type of clutter and is crucial to understand what needs to exist instead of clutter. Your brain is an amazing organ and can be a great support system when the clarity of the final goal is available. Target state is a specific, measurable and actionable scenario that you need to get to, in order to achieve the desired result.

You need to identify why you are doing the elimination and what will be achieved at the end of it. If you have an upcoming house inspection of your rented property versus guests coming to visit your place, the cleaning needs to be done in both the cases; however, the objective of the cleaning changes. For house inspection, the place needs to be neat and tidy to show that you are taking good care of the property and highlight all the repairs that need to be done by the owner or agent. In the case of guests visiting, the house needs to be cleaned to make it feel welcoming and comfortable to the guest, which might require you to take extra notice of things that need repairing so that guest aren't affected or concerned by it.

Step 3: Progressive approach vs. big-bang approach

Some elimination needs to be done over time while others can be done all at once, like a big bang. Throwing away an old cable is easy, and you just need to pack those electronics away in the electronics recyclable bin. Getting rid of old furniture may take some time as you might decide to sell them second hand. Same applies for other clutter as well; starting to work out in the evening and after sunset required me to adjust my body through consistent training over months.

Social and psychological clutter requires progressive change to become sustainable. We need consistent actions over a long period of time. Trying to achieve this in one go can do more harm than benefit and might also lead to unnecessary overwhelm and stress.

Step 4: Take the action

Remember the golden rule: All the planning in the world will get you nowhere if you don't take the necessary action. After deciding to eliminate clutter, you need to identify and take the actions. Also, you need to decide the sequence of actions needed to reach the desired state. This will involve consistency and clarity about why you are doing what you are doing and how and when it needs to be done. Once clarity is achieved, you need to build momentum by starting small and staying consistent.

In the next chapter, we are going to learn how to make productivity a part of day-to-day life, how to leverage the power of habits and routines to ensure things become so easy they don't require conscious effort.

In short

1. Decision fatigue, high need for variety, focusing on wants instead of needs and procrastination designed for presumed failure can lead to overwhelm.
2. Elimination allows you to focus your energy and effort on necessary actions and remove those that do not serve the purpose.
3. You can eliminate clutter by
    a. Identifying clutter.
    b. Deciding the target state.
    c. Adopting a progressive approach for clutters that cannot be eliminated immediately.
    d. Taking the necessary action.

CHAPTER 9

ELEVATE: THE SUB-CONSCIOUS PARADIGM

I still remember taking driving lessons for the first time. As a family, we did not own a car and the only time I had experienced travelling in a car was in the passenger seat. As I started taking lessons for driving the car, I became aware about all the display and dials on the car, the functions of the clutch, brake and accelerator, how to hold the steering wheel in the ten and two formation, how to set the rear view mirror and side mirrors, adjust seat height and keep an eye on road signs, being vigilant while driving on the road and following all the rules. The first drive was overwhelming, and even though I knew what needed to be done (as instructed by driving instructor), I could not keep track of everything.

There were many starts, stops, pauses and restarts! Luckily, I was driving in a secluded place, otherwise I would have surely met an accident. As I took more lessons and stayed consistent in practise, the application of driving skills became easier, and I could earn my license and drive without any instruction. Now, I can drive without even thinking consciously, sometimes even listening to a song or having small chat with passengers and still be able to perform all the driving actions and stay vigilant on the road. This is because I have reached a level of proficiency where things do not need conscious thinking. This is the level I aspired to when I took that first lesson.

As a working professional, whether in your job or as a business owner, you had to start somewhere. However, as you kept putting consistent effort into the task at hand, things started becoming easier. If you are feeling overwhelmed, the reason is you have so much to do and simply cannot keep track of all the pending tasks and actions. Your mind is working in overdrive to ensure safety, efficiency and results while trying to follow the rules of the game. As the responsibilities grow, so does the energy required to fulfil those responsibilities. The idea is to ensure we never run out of energy while accomplishing everything that needs to be done. The secret is to **elevate** ourselves to the level of a professional, accomplishing tasks and handling responsibilities with consistency and efficiency with minimal effort.

> *You don't become professional through a designation or a title. You become professional when you become consistent in performance and results.*

What differentiates a professional athlete from a novice is the consistency of results and efforts. The professional athlete has more clarity of what needs to be done to get the intended performance on a consistent basis, while a novice is just getting started and needs lots of training and coaching to become consistent in effort and results. Professionals have learned how to ensure their energy is directed at things that give them advantages during the competition. They have a mindset that sets them apart from the crowd. They perform physical feats that look almost impossible for a normal human to achieve.

So far as a part of D.O.N.E. framework, we have learned how to maximize our variable E by using these methods:

Dissociate: Step back and engage logical thinking to analyse and look at problems, situations and scenarios from the third persons point of view.

Own: Identify your responsibilities and actions and focus energy only on those actions.

Nudge: Eliminate friction and remove clutter that stops progress.

In the **elevate** step, we are going to explore how to leverage the power of our subconscious mind to make productivity feel effortless and elevate our behaviour and mindset to achieve our intended results consistently.

In the Chapter 2, I did mention how your brain will always choose the path of least resistance, and therefore you find it very difficult to break old patterns and habits. This tendency of the brain can be used as a tool.

Tools are the instruments which aid specific actions. How you use the tools determine whether the tool is going to help you or not. This tendency of the brain is also helpful in making tough things feel effortless when habits and routines are developed to make actions subconscious.

'The subconscious mind is more powerful than the conscious mind. It is the seed of all memory and emotional responses and directs over 90% of our behaviour.' - Dr. Joseph Murphy, The Power of Your Subconscious Mind (1963)

You might feel that the subconscious mind driving over 90% of our behaviour sounds excessive. Let me elaborate with an example. When you wake up on any normal day: you move your body in a certain way to get up from the bed, stand on your feet, stretch to feel relaxed, go for a morning routine like brushing your teeth, washing your face, preparing and sipping morning coffee or tea and do what you always do. No one is guiding you to do any of these actions. The decisions are on autopilot. This is your subconscious mind, operating on the principle of the path of least resistance. If learnt in the past, the subconscious mind will repeat the steps without letting you spend energy on making choices. You don't need to learn how to brush every morning or consciously think how many times you need to brush each of your teeth, how to put on clothes or how to wear your shoes; they happen automatically. The only time you actually think consciously is when you have to make choices, such as which dress to wear or which shoes go with which outfit, whether to go to work or not (based on the day of the week) and even whether to set an alarm to get up at a particular time or let yourself wake up naturally.

Even though it looks straight forward (consciously we choose, and subconsciously we just repeat the learned ways of performing tasks), this is not always the truth. What we have learned also affects how we consciously make choices and live our lives through filters, patterns and behaviours.

To **elevate** means to leverage this power of subconscious so that the first three steps become effortless (we leverage logical thinking when looking at any situation, problem or scenario, we identify our ownership of the actions without wasting our attention on energy vampires, we remove friction and declutter our life all on the autopilot mode).

Let's explore how we can leverage this superpower to **elevate**.

1. Repetition, Repetition, Repetition

The human brain learns from repetition. What we repeat on a consistent basis becomes our habits. The conscious mind uses analytical thinking and logical reasoning to look at every scenario, weigh pros and cons and make decisions. Our subconscious mind, on the other hand, uses learned behaviours, existing patterns and repeated exposures. In layman's terms, what we get used to doing and seeing becomes normal and acceptable for our subconscious. For example, if I ask you what monkeys eat, the default answer, even without thinking, is bananas, because we have been exposed to the image of a monkey eating a banana all our lives.

The subconscious will still prefer to choose the default answer, even if we acquire new knowledge. For instance, if I ask you to fill in this blank, the sun rise in the _________ direction. The default answer is 'east', something that we learn since kindergarten. This is contradictory to the knowledge that sun neither rise nor sets; earth rotates around its axis, causing night and day patterns based on which face of the earth is facing the sun. That may be the factually true answer, but the quick, default and no energy answer is going to be what we have learned subconsciously through repetition. The same is also applicable for our behaviours. If you get triggered whenever a situation becomes challenging, this can also be attributed to learned behaviours and patterns. By adopting conscious repetition of an alternate behaviour (**dissociate**, **nudge** and **own**), you can change how to approach such situations in the future.

When faced with a situation that seems difficult, dissociate and ask yourself, 'Is this the reality or a trained behaviour triggered by my subconscious mind?' If it is reality, then engage your third person point of view to identify the key variables, followed by identifying high-impact actions. This needs to be followed by determining the ownership of those actions. When done on a repeated basis, this pattern will become your default behaviour. Every time you practise it, you choose to create subconscious patterns in your brain.

2. Using a Reset Ritual

Many athletes have rituals before starting a race or a match. This involves a self-talk, mantra, music or just a series of actions they perform to get into a focused mindset. You, as a working professional or business owner, face many instances within a day when a challenge is provided to you, making you think and identify steps to resolve the issue. When these issues cascade, your energy levels also get depleted quickly. Having a reset ritual in these scenarios is key for not allowing different challenges to add on pressure and helping you tackle each one individually. It can be as simple as taking a deep breath or counting from one to ten before jumping from one task to another.

3. Emotional Anchors

Another tool that is very useful and is backed by neuroscience is using emotional anchors. Neuro-linguistic programming defines emotional anchoring as a process of linking your emotional state with any sensory trigger, such as smell, taste, sound or visual cues. For example, a red traffic light signals your brain to press brakes of the vehicle, and the green one indicates accelerate, the sound of rain drops or ocean waves triggers relaxation, the smell and taste of a warm cookie triggers joy, etc. These associated emotions with a picture, music, smell or taste are examples of your subconscious being trained to respond in the default mode and trigger an emotional response. Identify the anchors that can be used. Some of the emotional anchors are listed below:

- Auditory anchors (sound and music)

Many athletes listen to a specific playlist just before getting ready for a game or a race. You can create a playlist of songs or sounds that get you motivated and super focused just before starting work, such as a song that instantly brings back a fond memory, e.g. your wedding song or a childhood favourite, the sound of ocean waves to trigger calmness and peace or applause to trigger confidence or a sense of achievement.

Also, recorded or spoken phrases can act as a reminder that you can solve any problem. These can be words of encouragement or motivation. For me the statement "it is simple when you know how to do it" has become a mantra of sorts that gets me into a curious mindset and triggers my analytical rigour. The precaution that needs to be taken here is using it as a starting point only and not have it playing in the background. Otherwise, an additional dependency is created, and you might find yourself procrastinating things when this playlist is missing.

- Olfactory anchors (smell)

A particular smell can also trigger emotions in you. Ask any smoker who is trying to get rid of a smoking habit what the smell of lit cigarette does to them. This can be used to trigger positive emotion as well (e.g. smell of coffee, scented candle or perfume).

- Visual anchors

These are physical object that can be viewed. I have a gym bag I purchased six years ago. It is a small, blue one. Every time I pick up the bag, my body feels ready to hit the gym, and energy surges. I once picked up the bag just before going to sleep by mistake and struggled to fall asleep as it triggered incorrect emotions. So, you need to be careful when creating these anchors. Some other examples can be colours, a picture as a desktop background or on worktable.

- Kinaesthetic anchors

These are my favourites as they work on deeper level.

> *Our physiology affects our psychology.*

The concept of a 'power pose', introduced and popularized by social psychologist Amy Cuddy, along with colleagues Dana R. Carney and Andy Yap, in a 2010 paper published in the journal *Psychological Science*, states that by having an open stance imitating a gorilla or a bear, you increase your testosterone level, triggering blood flow to limbs and creating a confidence surge. Clenching your fist with raised hands or making "V" shape with fingers while visualizing success is also commonly used by athletes.

- Verbal/thought anchors

Some examples of verbal or thought anchors are: A phrase or self-talk that triggers calm (e.g., 'I've handled worse'). Hearing your name spoken in a kind tone, evoking warmth or connection. Replaying a compliment in your head to feel encouraged. A nickname someone used that reminds you of your identity in that relationship. A prayer or affirmation repeated often that brings peace or power.

4. Channelling focus

We have discussed how our brains filter out information into conscious and subconscious channels, avoiding sensory overwhelm. This is the basis of our reality. And we are equipped with a powerful tool to reshape and reform our reality—our focus and attention.

'Where focus goes, energy flows.' - Tony Robbins

Let's take an example. Imagine you are traveling to work and your car (if you own one) is not working, so you decide to take public transport. After reaching your workplace you realise you forgot your mobile phone on the public transport (this is based on a real situation I have been through last year while travelling to work).

Once realisation sets in, there are multiple things that can happen. By answering the following two questions, let's explore.

Question 1: What can it mean?

I lost a phone and may not get it back. I will lose the contact details of my friends, family and colleagues and other professional contacts. I might need to buy a new phone. A stranger can try to access my data on the phone. I am a forgetful person. I was not careful in keeping my phone with me. I was distracted by my thoughts. I will be late to work, and my boss will get angry, and so on.

Question 2: What else it could mean?

I will need to contact the authorities and try to get the phone back. I had mobile phone safety pin and security code, so my data is safe. I will not be distracted by social media and finally can have some time for myself. I learnt a lesson: I need to be more careful while traveling and keep my stuff safe. I will inform my boss, friends and colleagues that I have lost my phone. I will focus my energy and time on finding my phone.

In these answers, there are two reactions on the opposite side of the reflection spectrum: The first scenario is on the effect side, and second one is on the cause/action side. Both are valid and natural; however, which answer you focus on will determine your emotions and the resultant energy you carry throughout the day. What you chose to focus on will ultimately determine how you carry yourself for the next two or three hours or even longer. I have lost my phone three times in the past, twice in Mumbai and once in Sydney, a few years apart, and one thing became very clear: What I focused on determined my mood and energy levels for the next few hours.

Let's take another example: Imagine you get into an accident and as a result suffer a fracture of the right foot needing a couple of months for recovery.

Question 1: What can it mean?

You will need to rely on crutches to walk. You will need to take break from sports or rapid movement. You will miss work while treatment is being done. You will have to have a few visits to the doctor's office. It can lead to pain and physical discomfort and so on.

Question 2: What else it could mean?

You will finally take a break from your fast-paced life. Your friends and family members will most likely get in touch with you to check on your progress. With reduced movement, you can spend time reading those books, learning that guitar, re-connecting with a lost connection through your phone and other things you always wanted to do. You will receive treatment and can help someone in the future through your experience.

Again, the recovery of the fractured foot is going to take similar effort and time, and there will be practical implications. What you focus on, however, will change the quality of experience you have during this recovery.

Our education system has trained us to focus mostly on what is lacking or our weaknesses, for instance, particular academic subjects that we are not good at, skills that need enhancement and shortcomings that need to be overcome to reach an acceptable standard (so-called). This has trained our subconscious minds to focus on what needs to be corrected and what is wrong, ignoring the aspect "What else it could mean?" This gets carried into our adult life as well. When you are given feedback either at the year-end performance review or from the clients or customer, it is natural tendency to only focus on what was highlighted as a shortcoming. The feedback might include many positive things, but the brain tends to focus on what was said as a shortcoming or improvement opportunity.

I am not saying you should not give attention to improvement opportunities; however, maintaining and improving the variable E requires us to take both aspects of the feedback. By using these two simple questions, you can develop resilient mindset to improve and manage variable E better.

When you focus on both aspects of any scenario or situation, you are training your subconscious to become more accommodating and support you in making progress and overcoming limitations that you might have unintentionally created for yourself.

5. Add the element of fun

Since childhood, fun has been considered an enemy of focus and concentration, something that causes distractions and acts as an interruption. This was partially true in cases where fun was dependent on external sources, such as playing with friends, watching TV and playing video games. But on the days when fun became part of the process, progress became super easy. I was never good at remembering stuff; learning by heart was a concept I struggled with the most. The subject of history was my nemesis. I had to remember so many dates, events and locations. However, there was a particular event, the stories of which were told to me by my father. That one was easy; I loved listening and remembering stories of that event in the past and therefore, that particular event was fun to learn about even in books.

When I told my father about this particular event, he casually said, 'Why don't you learn rest of the history like a story?' and suddenly history was a fun subject. Fun is an element that can make any task feel like a breeze. A person who enjoys dancing is not worried about the effort needed to move the body. For a person enjoying fishing, sitting at one place is a serene experience. For an avid shopper, shopping for hours does not tire the legs. The element of fun ensures your energy levels are not depleted; rather, they are refilled.

When you are having fun, boredom simply vanishes. Dopamine levels are spiked, and you get into the flow state or zone very easily. So how do you involve fun in your daily routines and tasks? You don't need to change the task, just the way you do it.

- Gamification: You can convert any task into a game. For example, if you have to write a report you despise, for every 50 words you write you can give yourself 10 points and once you get 500 points, you will earn a reward such as 5 minutes of social media scrolling or a bite of dark chocolate.

- Change your environment: Add fun elements such as a small punching bag or a stress ball to squeeze, light up the location, have colours added that stimulate your mind, have a special bouncing chair or foot massager near your desk that you use when dealing with tedious tasks.

- Inject creativity into the task itself: Use colours, silly names, sticky notes with funny jokes, fancy pens, a mini trampoline, and others.

You don't have to make your whole life a party. The goal isn't to be silly but to become strategic in using fun to make tasks feel effortless. The objective here is to make progress seems effortless and make the journey as enjoyable as the result.

For a quick recap, so far, we have learnt how to do the following:

1. Dissociate from any situation and scenario to capture all the key variables at play.
2. Take ownership of what is actionable.
3. Remove the friction by decluttering.
4. Create a support system that nudges you into action.
5. Leverage your sub-conscious to elevate your mindset on a sustainable basis by using reset rituals, the power of repetition and channelling focus, things that support your energy levels.

You also learnt why you are unique and must align your actions based on what works for you as per your value systems and styles.

In the next chapter you will learn a concept of the D.O.N.E. framework that makes making progress sustainable, adds consistency in your life and ensures failure becomes almost impossible.

In short

1. Subconscious mind drives over 90% of human behaviour.
2. You need to elevate your new learned behaviour to the subconscious level by using:
    a. Repetition.
    b. Reset ritual.
    c. Emotional anchors.
    d. Two questions (what can it mean? and what else it could mean?) and channelling your focus.
    e. Element of fun.

CHAPTER 10

RULES OF FAILURE: THE SUCCESS INSURANCE

Success and results are not always directly proportional. I have seen many individuals who were lacking results in the short run but kept going forward, adding incremental progress and ultimately reaching a stage which was not the initial goal, but something even better. On the other hand, the following pattern is very common amongst individuals who struggle to break habits that are not serving them.

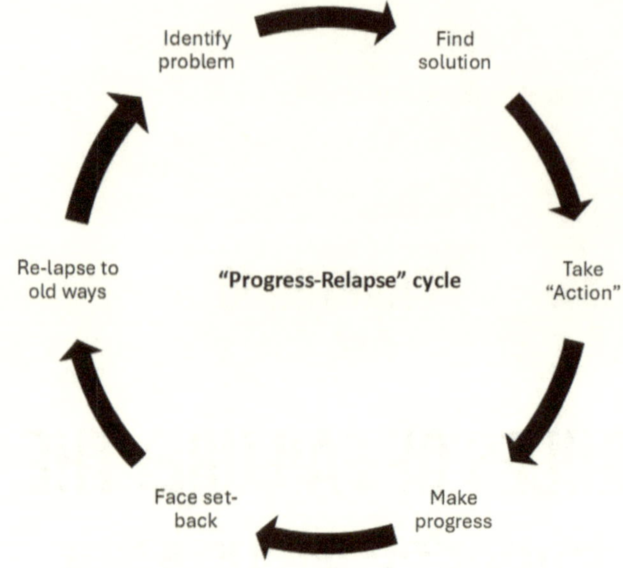

You decided to make the change, you identified the problem, you took necessary action and made progress. After some time, due to setbacks or circumstances, you go back to old ways, completely forgetting what you learned, and as the time goes on, you start searching for new ways to solve the problem, and the cycle continues. I like to refer it as 'progress-relapse' cycle.

This pattern is not new. It is applicable to different scenarios and even when dealing with addiction. Relapse is not a crime; it is a way for your brain and subconscious mind to seek familiarity and follow known patterns. It is like going to the ice cream shop on a hot summer afternoon and choosing that one ice cream you always have, despite all the new flavours being introduced in the catalogue. This is a sign that you are still living in survival mode, and when your safety is threatened, subconsciously you want to feel safe and stop that tingling feeling of discomfort, seeking that short term dopamine boost.

'There is no failure except in no longer trying.'
- Chris Bradford (from The Way of the Sword)

In the field of analytics as well, the biggest struggle is not in finding solutions but in evolving and using new methods and technologies. If you are familiar with Microsoft Excel (it is ok if you aren't), learning the VLOOKUP function is required to develop the medium-to-advanced-level Excel skills. People need to learn how to use it and practise over a period to get used to it. However, the VLOOKUP function has its limitations, and therefore XLOOKUP was introduced back in 2019. But there are people who would still stick to VLOOKUP even after getting ample number of lessons in using XLOOKUP. Familiarity even at the cost of progress is the default mode for the subconscious mind.

Even the person with the best of resolve will relapse at times. Saying that, it doesn't mean we can never break the cycle, or that it needs herculean effort every time. As an analyst, I have learnt one thing: 'If a problem exists, there has to be a solution'. A different approach is needed for the sustainability issue. For an instance, in a multiple-choice question paper with four options, if you don't know the correct answer, you have a 75% chance of failure (3 out of 4 options are incorrect). To improve your chance of success, you can choose to eliminate the obvious wrong answers first, reducing options from possible 4 to possible 2 (a 50% chance of failure) and then focus your energy in identifying the correct answer amongst the two options left. Even if you take a guess, the probability of success has gone up.

In day-to-day life, we do not get multiple choice questions every time, and answers are vague and need thinking from scratch. To improve the chances of success in the real world, you need to define the 'rules of failure'.

You might think, why do you need rules of failures? There are enough rules created by people for success; are we regressing? Actually, no.

This is because success and failure are inversely proportional to each other, which means as one goes up, the other goes down. It is difficult to imagine for some, as they have always thought of success being the opposite of failure. It is not binary in nature (binary meaning either 0 or 1—if it exists then it is equal to 1, if not it is equal to 0). Success and failure are like a see-saw, when one goes up, the other goes down. In mathematics it is called a scale, and there are moments in life when you are not at either end of the scale but somewhere in between. Ask any successful individual in their field of operation, and they will confirm they have seen enough failures before reaching a tipping point where success becomes overwhelmingly dominant, and the frequency of failure keeps on reducing

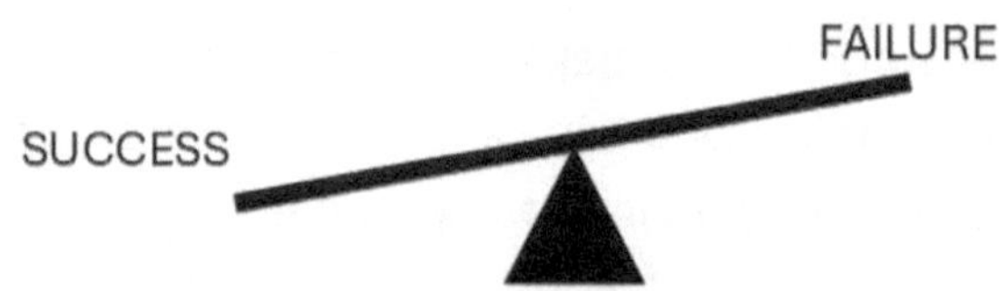

When you define the rules of failure, you are giving your brain clarity on parameters that needs to be met before you declare failure. This helps in overcoming the all-or-nothing mentality and stopping you from throwing away all the progress you have made in the process, breaking the progress-relapse cycle.

Rules of failure play a pivotal role in taking away comparison as well. Everyone operates at a different frequency; some reach their goals within the stipulated timeline, and some take longer. In the world, where organizations have been mandated to create and publish their financial reports every quarter and justify every minute deviation, we also get trained to believe if we fail to reach targets within stipulated deadlines, then all our efforts have been a waste. It is easier for the brain to get fogged by imaginary demons than to face the reality that time is man-made construct. Our ancestors survived and made progress even before calendars existed. Monthly, quarterly and annual deadlines are for accounting purposes, and they do create hurdles at times because we forget the core purpose of timelines and target dates: to help us evaluate our progress against a benchmark.

When you have chosen an action or a goal, you need to be clear in terms of what parameters you set to declare it a failure so that minor setbacks do not make you throw away all the progress. It also helps you in overcoming fear of failure, because it is easier to deal with a known devil than an unknown monster. When you know exactly what will make you fail, it becomes simpler for you to take steps to avoid it at all costs. This works wonders for the people who have avoidance of failure/punishment as a subconscious driving force.

For example, if someone decides to improve their health by working out regularly, the person needs to consider and calculate the possibility of missing out on workout for few days due to reasons such as sickness, a family emergency, work priority and others.

Resistance is highest when getting started and restarting after momentum is broken.

I loved working out regularly during my MBA days, and after I joined an organization for work, I wanted to continue the same lifestyle. I enjoyed going to the gym, but I was posted in a remote location as the head of a regional distribution centre. I had to travel one-and-a-half hours each way daily to reach my office, work throughout the day for six days a week, sometimes even late hours. There was no gym nearby. I ended up purchasing two 7 kg dumbbells for working out at home and decided to go for a run on days I could squeeze in some time. Initially, I was consistent with my goals. Then the financial year-end came, and due to multiple deadlines and mandatory activities, working hours became even longer. I was working 14 hours each day for few weeks, and additional travel time squeezed out any possibility of rest. I was exhausted and overwhelmed. Even after things settled down, my momentum was broken. I could not continue my workouts or runs. After few months of procrastination, I decided to restart my workout till the work stress got in the way again, causing a temporary halt, breaking the momentum, followed by period of no workouts. I found myself in the progress-relapse cycle.

This is where I defined rules of failure: I will only stop working out if I am not able to get at least a 10-minute run or touch my dumbbells for 3 straight days. This way, even when I could not get a full 30-minute workout, I ensured, every time I had at least 10 minutes in a day, I would squeeze in a small workout, even if it meant shifting one 7 kg dumbbell from one place to another in my room. So, when the busy phase stopped, I had not broken the momentum, and I could continue doing 30-minute workouts. It also took away the resistance needed on getting started and kept my goal in check, giving me much-needed exercise to manage my busy life.

This also helped me in writing this book, because my rule of failure was this: 'I am successfully progressing in completing my book if at least once in a week, I write at least 20 words.' This got me going, and I continued working way past my twenty-word limit, eventually completing this book.

The rule of failure needs you to focus on the bare minimum progress needed to keep the ball moving, things ticking, building momentum and avoiding resistance. For activities that cause overwhelm such as not resting well, scheduling kids during school holidays, never ending to-do list, if you have identified actions through the D.O.N.E framework, identifying a rule of failure for that action will do wonders in making steady progress.

Remember, we are humans, not machines, and our energy levels fluctuate on a daily basis. Even if we plan our lives meticulously, ensuring there is no resistance and things are always running smoothly, we cannot expect the same performance every time. Even the best athletes in the world have off days. Showing up every day doesn't guarantee the same level of performance every day. However, doing the bare minimum, if that is what is possible, keeps you moving forward.

'It does not matter how slowly you go as long as you do not stop.' - Confucius

Saying that, you also need to keep this in mind: you should not confuse movement with progress. If the intended actions are not giving you results even on peak performance days and you have given those actions enough time, it might be necessary to take a pause and re-assess. In defining rules of failure, you identified the action and stayed consistent. What if the progress is still missing? In this case, you need to show flexibility and identify the alternate action using **dissociate** step of the D.O.N.E. framework.

There is also a quick method backed by neuro-linguistic programming, which helps you quickly arrive at the alternate action.

Identify the Higher Purpose of the Action

When you decide on a resolution or a goal, it has a higher purpose. This purpose can sometimes be hidden or sometimes be visible in disguise. In fact, every action you perform has a higher purpose. The simple act of driving a car can lead to variety of higher purposes. These are identified by asking a simple question:

> *'What is the purpose of this action?'*

Repeat the question three times to identify the alternates. For the example of driving a car, a few answers I have received from my clients are provided below:

Client 1:

What is the purpose of driving a car?
- To get to a destination

What is the purpose of getting to a destination?
- To meet other people

What is the purpose of meeting other people?
- To build relationships

Client 2:

What is purpose of driving a car?
- To travel from one place to another

What is the purpose of travelling from one place to another?
- To finish work

What is the purpose of finishing work?
- To be at peace

Client 3:

What is the purpose of driving a car?
- To get away from a place

What is the purpose of getting away from a place?
- To escape boredom

What is the purpose of escaping boredom?
- To have fun

In the above three examples, the starting question remains the same, but after asking three times the purpose of the answers three times, you get the different answers based on individuals' higher purpose of the action or goal.

The reason to find the higher purpose is to look at other options available because if one path fails, the alternate options can be chosen by simply asking, 'What are the other ways I could meet the higher purpose?'

Let us assume you are feeling overwhelmed because you have a never-ending email list. The identified step to resolve it was to categorize each email as actionable or non-actionable before even going into the details of it. This worked for some time, but still the emails are never-ending. You need to identify alternate solutions. Let's explore the higher purpose.

What is the purpose of answering email?
- To share critical information

What is the purpose of sharing critical information?
- To inform key stakeholders of needed actions

What is the purpose of informing key stakeholders of needed actions?
- To ensure critical tasks are done

Focusing on the higher purpose of ensuring critical tasks are done, many emails can be converted into a shared google document or another format that can be shared between key stakeholders, where regular updates can be shared, and missing out on critical information can be avoided. This will reduce the amount of time required for you to check each individual email at random times. I am not saying this is the only solution, but knowing the higher purpose allows you to think about the alternatives that will help resolve the problem causing you to reach overwhelm. Many companies have dashboards where all critical business updates are automatically refreshed, and some of the reports are in the format where individual stakeholders can customize information as per need. This optimizes time spent on communication to the key stakeholders.

Once you have defined rules of failure, it becomes simpler to sustain your actions and let you repeat the same till it becomes part of your subconscious. This also helps you develop a mindset of clarity, consistency and concrete steps to create long-lasting, sustainable benefits, elevating your performance and breaking the progress-relapse cycle.

At this point, it is possible you might think this is lot of information, and it might feel difficult to keep track of all the steps and apply them on a regular basis. You were promised a simple framework, but it doesn't feel simple. As the saying goes, 'Chaos often precedes clarity'. It is natural to feel the clarity is still not there. So far, we have covered the details of each step of the D.O.N.E. framework and learned examples of how it can be useful.

In the next chapter we are going to look at the D.O.N.E. framework from an implementation perspective, where the analyst in me, who loves to simplify things, takes over. So, buckle up, because now we go to the chapter where all the magic happens.

In short

1. The 'progress-relapse cycle' is very common, and rules of failure help you break it.
2. Success and failure are like a seesaw and therefore as one goes up, the other goes down.
3. Define a rule of failure to identify bare minimum criteria that you can satisfy to maximise the chances of success and maintain the momentum and progress.
4. By identifying higher purpose of the action, you can quickly identify the alternate action if the initially identified action is not giving intended benefits.

CHAPTER 11

D.O.N.E. PRACTICALLY: FROM THEORY TO REALITY

Congratulations on making it so far. In the previous chapters, we learned in detail the different aspects of the D.O.N.E framework and how to apply and use the different steps. It is natural to feel that I've provided too much information, and it is very difficult to keep track of all the steps and actions. This is where simplification becomes necessary. Let me give you a quick simple summary of the D.O.N.E. framework.

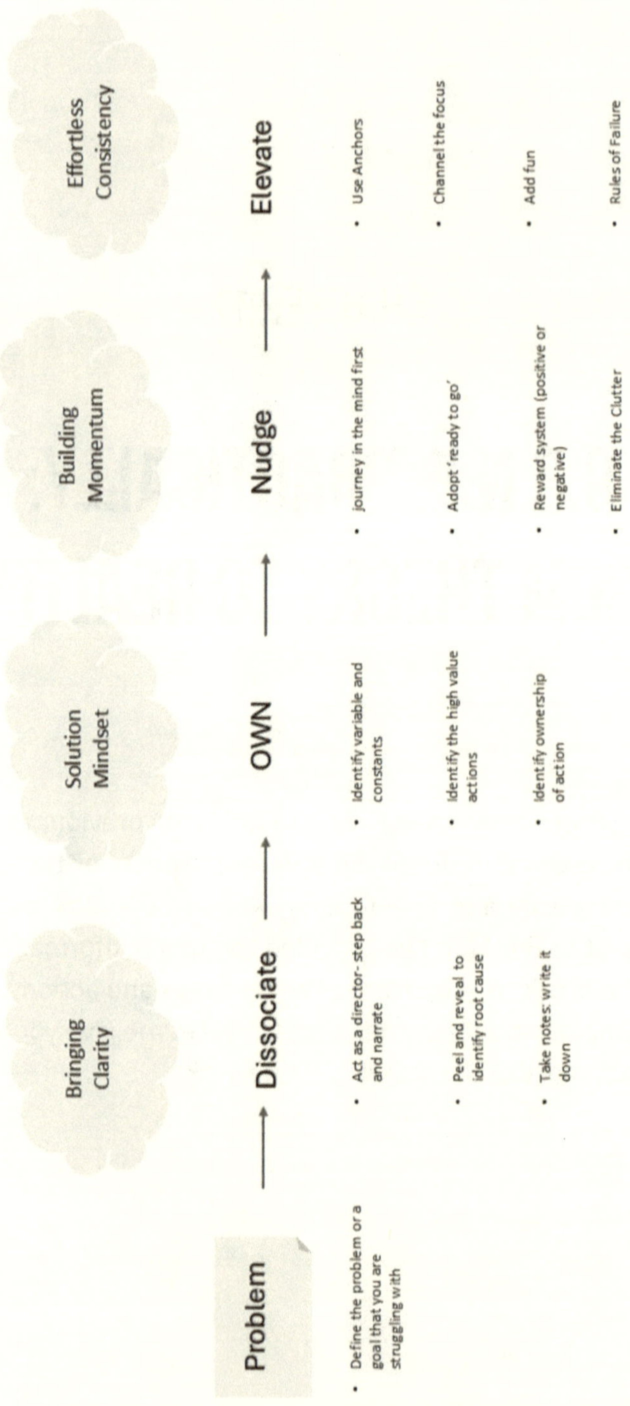

Problem	→ Dissociate	→ OWN	→ Nudge	→ Elevate
	Bringing Clarity	Solution Mindset	Building Momentum	Effortless Consistency
• Define the problem or a goal that you are struggling with	• Act as a director- step back and narrate	• Identify variable and constants	• journey in the mind first	• Use Anchors
	• Peel and reveal to identify root cause	• Identify the high value actions	• Adopt 'ready to go'	• Channel the focus
	• Take notes: write it down	• Identify ownership of action	• Reward system (positive or negative)	• Add fun
			• Eliminate the Clutter	• Rules of Failure

Once you look at the D.O.N.E. framework in the summarized format, it becomes simple to visualize and remember.

Since the D.O.N.E. framework is designed to create long lasting solutions that work for you, let's identify your uniqueness for practical implementation purposes. Please select the option in the last column that describes you the best. In case you have difficulty in choosing the option for any characteristic, remember to choose the option which will describe you when you are at your most comfortable, away from work or a professional set-up as that is your natural way of functioning.

This will help you identify your unique style and create a solution that works for you the best. This is necessary because if the solution identified for you to resolve the issue is against your identified operating style, you might need to put in a lot more energy (variable E) as forming new patterns and behaviours will need undoing years of subconscious training. It also provides clarity when choosing the best option to resolve the issue (during OWN steps), because the identified option which is in line with your characteristics often gives sustainable solutions in the longer run.

Characteristics	Option a	Option b	Your answer (a or b)
Motivation	Love of reward (better the prize, more motivated)	Fear of Punishment (Rather safe than sorry)	
Thinking style	Linear Thinker (love steps, structure and consistent progress)	Non-Linear Thinker (Go with flow)	
Inner clock	Through time (love keeping track of time)	In-time (get lost in the zone and need reminders)	
Energy Peak	Early riser (most active earlier in the day)	Late bloomers (peak later in the day- afternoon or evenings)	
Learning style	Instruction based (Need guidance and training)	Kinaesthetic (Figure out by self)	
Driven by	Results (Outcome matters over feelings and convenience of other)	Relationship (Feelings and convenience of other matters more than results)	
Speed	Faster is Better	Slow and Steady	

The two interrelated problems that you want to tackle and solve with the D.O.N.E. framework are overwhelm and procrastination. The best way to deal with them is through gaining clarity and overcoming inertia to build momentum. The **dissociate** and **own** steps of the D.O.N.E. framework help you in getting the needed clarity to get a wholistic view of the problem and catch the pulse and get to the core issue. The **nudge** step helps you in removing resistance and hurdles by identifying the clutter and psychological biases. The **elevate** step makes "taking action" consistent and engages the subconscious mind to make progress effortless. In short, the first two steps of **dissociate** and **own** are designed to help you arrive at practical solutions, and the steps of **nudge** and **elevate** are to make the solutions sustainable.

Once you have identified your unique style, the next step is to define the problem.

Step 1: Identify concern/problem

Write down the problem you are facing on a piece of paper or on any digital platform. You can also take a verbal note through recording. Provide as many details as possible and also mention how it affects you emotionally.

Once you have completed this step, you have brought the problem out of your head and into the real world.

Outcome of this step: Situation/Concern in written format

Step 2: Dissociate (D)

   a. Director's voice (third person POV)

Now take the problem and re-frame it in third person point of view. Replace all the pronouns (I, He, She, It etc) with symbolic names such as person A, person B, location X, company Y, thing no.1, thing no 2 etc. Also, use passive voice as much as possible. This is to ensure the emotional attachment is removed from the problem/ concern identified.

After this, take a 15-minute break (or longer) and do not look at the problem during this time. If you can take a small walk, that is even better as it involves your physiology as well. This allows brain to rest and create a physical distance from the issue/concern at hand.

   b. Peel and reveal

If you are a linear thinker, use the Pattern Log Recognition method, and if you are non-linear thinker use 5 Why technique to identify the core issue and differentiate from the surface level symptoms.

Once you have identified the core issue, re-write the concern/issue in the form of a problem statement.

Outcome of this step: Problem statement:

Step 3: OWN (O)

a. Variables and constants: In the problem statement identify all the involved variables (things that can change) and constants (things that cannot change in the short run).

List of Variables	List of constants

b. Brainstorming to identify high value actions: Identify all the possible actions that can help you solve the issue/concern at hand. Do not judge any of the actions. Everything and anything possible under the sun is considered.

List all possible actions

c. Shortlist the top action: This action, when taken, should resolve the issue at hand completely.

    (p.s. you might feel you need to take more than one action to completely resolve the issue, focus on top 1 at the moment and come back to action 2 and 3 later. This will help you channel the focus and not get distracted. Also, keep in mind your uniqueness and identified style of operation. You don't want to prioritize the action that goes completely against your natural style. E.g. if are not an early riser, do not make getting up at 5 am everyday your top action. This will decrease the probability of your success by making action very difficult to sustain in the long run.)

d. Stakeholders and ownership: Identify all the stakeholders involved in accomplishing the high-value action and assign ownership. Have the necessary conversation and arrangements for the action you cannot control and then channel your energy and focus on the actions that are under your control.

Outcome of this step: Identified high value action

Step 4: Nudge

a. Journey in the mind first: Do the journey in the mind first using the three possible scenarios to identify the possible friction and energy vampires.

    Best case scenario:

    Worst case scenario:

    Most likely scenario:

b. Adopt ready to go: Make necessary arrangements and preparation to minimize the effort that you need closer to the occurrence of the event. This can be done by identifying and eliminating clutter.

c. Design the reward system: Based on whether you are driven by love for reward or fear of punishment, create a reward system.

Outcome of this step: preparation steps to eliminate clutter and energy vampires

Step 5: Elevate

a. Add element of fun: Add fun to the activities by using emotional anchors or small things that make the activity fun for you.

b. Create rules of failure: Make failing in action almost impossible by creating bare minimum criteria to stop the progress relapse cycle. This will ensure you are always in the game and new actions help you achieve your higher purpose.

c. Repetition, repetition, repetition: Our sub-conscious learns from repetition, so keep making progress and repeat the identified action till it become part of your sub-conscious training.

d. Thank yourself: Do not forget to thank yourself for every step you take as it help sub-conscious create a positive support to ensure you keep making progress.

And remember to be flexible. In case all your efforts are still not giving the intended results, it is necessary to re-valuate the high action identified in OWN step of the D.O.N.E. framework as it might not have been the correct one. This is where you revisit the list of actions identified. You select the other action identified and repeat the remaining steps of D.O.N.E. framework.

By using the steps provided above you can implement the D.O.N.E. framework in your life and make sustainable and positive impact. The D.O.N.E. framework can also be used for goals and resolutions as I have identified the framework is effective and captures key elements for ensuring progress and making success sustainable without breaking the bank.

In short

1. By looking at the overall summary of the D.O.N.E. framework and following the steps, you can create solutions and actions that work for you.
2. If the progress is still missing, re-evaluate selected high-impact action during the Own step and follow the remaining steps of the D.O.N.E. framework.

CHAPTER 12

JUST GET IT D.O.N.E.

et me say something that is the most probable truth, as there is no absolute truth: You did not choose this book because you wanted inspiration or to re-learn what has been taught for ages. You wanted practical solutions to get ahead of the never-ending demand of busy work life, finish the unfinished goals, get rid of clutter that is causing overwhelm and make progress in life with sustainable solutions that do not break the bank. You wanted a way to kick out procrastination, to find a way out—not from work, but the burden and overwhelm that comes from work. And I want to congratulate you on making it to the end of the book.

The D.O.N.E. framework was never meant to be a quick fix or a one-size-fits-all solution; rather, it's a way to help you explore the journey of your fast-paced life through clarity, certainty and flexibility. You wanted to ride your bicycle of life on a concrete road and not through the mud of procrastination, slowing you down, making you overwhelmed. You wanted something that is easy to apply, giving sustainable solutions that have long-lasting impact.

You learned how to maximize the throughput of life by balancing the three key variables at play any time: the variable T (controllable time), the variable R (ability to gain resources) and variable E (energy). You also learned how to maximise your variable E (energy) to improve efficiency in daily work life.

You need to keep in mind the long-term drawbacks of operating under survival mode. The amygdala may not be hijacking your thinking all the time, but letting emotions control your actions will lead to build-up of long-term stress, which in turn affects your efficiency in managing your variable E. The simple step to keep yourself properly operating is to use the right kind of fuel to operate your body and mind. You only get one body, whether you like it or not, and till the field of biotechnology evolves to replace your physical organs or your body in its entirety, you need to use and maintain what you have been gifted, with all its strengths and weaknesses.

You don't need to train to climb Mount Everest; however, keeping enough fitness to operate without fatigue and having enough energy to fuel your actions without burning out is the need of the day. Your brain needs water and the right kind of calories. This is the simplest and smallest start you can do today. You wanted to get things D.O.N.E., so let's recap the framework one more time.

D is for **dissociate**, to take a step back and gain clarity on what is the core issue and how to become an objective observer, a director calling the shots instead of a distracted and overwhelmed actor. This makes you remove the emotional clutter, engage logical thinking and find clarity on what is the real issue at hand without getting distracted from symptoms.

O is for **ownership** of your actions and how to ensure your focus is on high-impact actions, eliminating anything that is non-actionable. It is not about doing more but doing what matters.

N is to **nudge** into action by identifying and removing friction, to prioritize *later* (the future) and act as your own personal assistant to help your future self. To identify the waste and declutter life. To ensure you build accountability and eliminate the excuses that stop progress.

E is to **elevate** by leveraging the tendency of the subconscious to adopt the path of least resistance, evolve routine and habits to make productivity effortless.

The D.O.N.E. framework is not about becoming a machine and being productive by hustling every second of the day but about taking back control and solving the problem of procrastination and overwhelm at its core. Our brain absorbs all the information, some of which is done consciously (~232 bits per second) and most subconsciously (2 billion bits per second). It is the repository of all the information that is needed to solve the problem. The main purpose of the D.O.N.E. framework is to let you utilise this capability and to guide it to bring out amazing solutions that solve the core issues.

So, what's next? Remember, if the knowledge is not applied, it is wasted. You need to apply the framework in real life. Take a goal that you have been procrastinating, an area of life where you feel overwhelmed, be it finances, personal health, your profession, your business, home life or anything else. Identify the challenges and the problems that need your action.

You don't need perfection; all you need is sustainable progress in the right direction, tackling the issues at their core and then channelling your focus on concrete actions.

'Life doesn't get easier; you just get stronger.'
- Steve Maraboli

The D.O.N.E. framework, when applied in real life, will give you actionable solutions that will work best for you. The actions will be automatically customized to fit your life, something you can embrace with your own personality. You become your own guide. It doesn't ask you to become someone else but instead requires you to embrace your own strengths and knowledge, act as your own best friend and give a solution that you know will solve your own problem. It allows you to remain authentic and true to yourself.

Next time you find yourself caught in the clutter of life, feeling overwhelmed by the never-ending challenges and procrastination, embrace the D.O.N.E. framework by telling yourself,

'Just get it done already!'

THREE OFFERS

Download your free D.O.N.E framework template resource

To help you get using and implementing the D.O.N.E framework in daily life, I have created an exclusive template for the D.O.N.E. framework, just for those who purchase this book.

I know that reading about a framework is one thing, but having it in front of you—simple, clear and ready to use—can be a game-changer. That's why I've created a special one-page D.O.N.E. Framework Guide called "D.O.N.E. at a glance" just for you, as a thank-you for picking up this book. Think of it as your pocket guide: a step-by-step reminder to Dissociate, Own, Nudge and Elevate whenever you feel stuck or overwhelmed. It's my way of making sure you don't just understand this system, but truly live it. You'll find the link and QR code inside—go ahead and grab your copy, and just get things D.O.N.E.

To download your guide, sign up here:

I'm also happy to help you with any of the procrastination or productivity questions you have. Please feel free to send me an e-mail at: contact@vishalpatil.com.au

You are welcome to visit my website https//vishalpatil.com.au for free resources and clarity tools to help you become best productive version of yourself.

SPEAKER BIO

Vishal Patil is a clarity and productivity coach with over 16 years of corporate experience across leadership, transformation, analytics and multicultural teams in Australia and Asia. With a background in engineering, an MBA and training in NLP and life coaching, Vishal blends sharp analytical thinking with a deep understanding of human behaviour.

Growing up in a small village in central India, Vishal's journey has shaped his grounded, relatable speaking style. His talks mix real-world experience, humour and practical tools that people can use immediately.

He speaks on clarity, procrastination, focus, energy management and the psychology behind truly getting things done. Known for turning complex ideas into simple, actionable insights, Vishal helps audiences rethink productivity—not as hustle, but as clarity-driven choices that create consistent progress.

Today, he works with professionals and teams to overcome overwhelm, cut through noise and perform at their productive best. Outside of work, he's a lifelong learner, sports lover and someone who grew up surrounded by animals—an upbringing that taught him empathy, resilience and the power of humble beginnings.

ABOUT THE AUTHOR

Vishal Patil was born and brought up in a small village in the central region of India, where curiosity and ambition shaped much of his early life. He went on to pursue an engineering degree, followed by an MBA, and later deepened his understanding of human behaviour by pursuing certifications in NLP and life coaching.

With over 16 years of corporate experience—including leadership, analytics and business transformation, and working in highly multicultural environments—Vishal brings practical, real-world insight into how people think, behave and get things done. He believes that clarity—not hustle—is the real engine of progress.

Today, he is a clarity coach and productivity mentor who helps professionals simplify their lives, beat procrastination and become their most productive selves. His work combines analytical thinking with practical psychology to make complex ideas feel simple, accessible and easy to apply in everyday life.

Vishal is passionate about sports, fitness, personal growth and animals. He is happily married and the proud father of a four-year-old, who constantly reminds him of the beauty of curiosity and play.

NOTES

www.ingramcontent.com/pod-product-compliance
Lightning Source LLC
Chambersburg PA
CBHW032030050726
47590CB00006B/2369